"What a treasure! My deep bow of gratitude to and for Shulamith for guiding us into this wealth of spirited and spiritual world readings. For how she gathers us to evening, rest, and sleep. For connecting us to the traditions of prayer and song. And listening to Divine Song: the earthly poetry inside our hearts."

—GARY MARGOLIS, author of *Museum of Islands: New and Selected Poems*

"As a Muslim who has encountered other faith traditions with an open heart due to being raised with an interfaith psyche, it is always a pleasure to meet a traveler on a similar path like Shulamith Clearbridge. Her book is an offering that such explorers dream of to share the heart-warming journey of not only self-discovery, but the realization of how much we are connected in our spirituality despite our apparent differences."

—S. ZAKIYA ISLAM, Adjunct Faculty, Temple University

"I recommend keeping *Good Night* beside your bed. It offers evocative questions to help us reflect on the day's experiences, encouraging us to notice how love was present and where we might have resisted grace-filled opportunities. Remembering and reflecting on our experiences helps us to 'settle the day' with greater receptivity to the divine presence in our daily lives. The book contains lessons, affirmations, and prayers for each night, wisdom from Quaker writers as well as from many other spiritual traditions, quotations that help us focus our minds and hearts on eternal truths as we prepare for sleep. This beautiful book invites us to rest in God all through the night and receive the blessings and spiritual guidance which are always available to us."

—MARCELLE MARTIN, author of *Our Life is Love: the Quaker Spiritual Journey*

"Shulamith Clearbridge offers a feast for the soul in this rich collection of readings and prayers meant to help us 'settle the day.' *Good Night* transposes the Christian spiritual practices of evening prayer and the *examen* into a refreshingly new key: By sourcing readings from many faiths and rendering them in gender-neutral language, Clearbridge makes these meditations accessible and inviting to a much wider audience. Providing forty days of readings and prayers on eleven different themes (such as gratitude, forgiving oneself, help and hope), *Good Night* covers a wide territory of the spirit that will leave you centered, settled, and ready for peaceful slumber and a fresh new day."

—Janet Parker, co-editor of *A Grounded Faith: Reconnecting with Creator and Creation in the Season of Lent*

"After an annoying and frustrating day, as I was getting ready for sleep, I opened *Good Night* and looked up the section on anger. The exercise of 'settling the day' let me look carefully at why I was annoyed. The lesson loosened the frustration in my heart. The affirmation and intention enabled me to let my irritation go. The prayer connected me with divine love. I slept well, resting in the Presence, and rose in the morning free to experience the blessings of a new day. I now use this book on any day, not only when I have a special need. Through *Good Night*, Shulamith has provided daily practices for deeper connection to the Source and better days."

—Joel D. Cook, Speaker and Workshop leader

"This book has become a trusted companion in my evening journaling practice. It's creatively structured in a way that's immensely helpful to this reader. Coming from a liberal Quaker background, I crave structure in my spiritual life and often have trouble finding it. Shulamith Clearbridge's expert pairings of settling queries, lessons, affirmations/intentions and prayers, allows me to sink into the words and the solace they bring. It's been lovely to find inspiration in such a wide array of thinkers and mystics, and I've enjoyed sitting with these quotes from both familiar and unfamiliar names. It's clear that Clearbridge searched far and wide for the wisdom in this book and knit it together with much thought and gentleness. In addition to the content, I was grateful for the different ways to read and use the book that Clearbridge offers in the introduction, and I have found myself returning to it for guidance often and enjoy experimenting with the different methods based on what I need in the moment. So grateful for this book! I've been especially grateful for the queries."

—OLIVIA CHALKLEY, The School of the Spirit Ministry

"For forty nights, you are invited to a spiritual practice of putting the day to rest. Shulamith provides a four-part practice: a reading or questions for reflection, a lesson, an intention or affirmation, and a prayer. The readings offer time to breathe and be present, time to process and sanctify the day, and an opportunity to rest in God. . . . With this book, Shulamith offers us a spiritual practice that people from all backgrounds and beliefs can benefit by. If you have ever come across a quote that stopped you in your tracks, a poem that painted truth with a capital 'T,' or a prayer that brought you to a deep place, this book is for you. Let Shulamith and these pages be a spiritual guide."

—JANAKI SPICKARD KEELER, Editor, Pendle Hill Publications

"How does one enter a night of rest? For years, it's been my journal and the current fiction I'm reading. This book, though, is giving me another idea: an intention of gently laying down the day, by reflecting, reading, and considering where my spirit might be inspired, mended, settled. This collection of writings from many faith traditions includes a roadmap of sorts—of emotional and experiential frames to consider, should there be a need to focus on one, as one seeks to settle the day. I am surprised at the welcome I feel—invited in. The inclusion of gender and God considerations in some of the adjusted language, even as the original is also included, feels warmly respectful and opening. This feels like a gift I never knew I needed."

—Joan Gunn Broadfield, Library Manager, Philadelphia Yearly Meeting

Good Night

Good Night

Interfaith Prayers and Meditations Before Sleep

SHULAMITH CLEARBRIDGE

RESOURCE *Publications* • Eugene, Oregon

GOOD NIGHT
Interfaith Prayers and Meditations Before Sleep

Resource Publications
An Imprint of Wipf and Stock Publishers
199 W. 8th Ave., Suite 3
Eugene, OR 97401

www.wipfandstock.com

PAPERBACK ISBN: 979-8-3852-6932-7
HARDCOVER ISBN: 979-8-3852-6933-4
EBOOK ISBN: 979-8-3852-6934-1

VERSION NUMBER 04/10/26

To my faithfulness group:

Joel Cook, Mary Igoe Meyers, Maryann Concannon, Paulette Meier

and

To the Coddiwomple Clearness Committee*

Without these dear, loving, wise, and steadfast friends,
I would not have become the person able to write this book.

*Coddiwomple: heading off purposefully towards an unknown or vague destination, while following Guidance

Contents

III. RESOURCES | 119

Permissions

"The Divine Milieu is a very personal and autobiographical book," from *On Hallowing One's Diminishments*, by John Yungblut, © 1990 by Pendle Hill Publications, reprinted by permission.

"Forgiveness is simply release into the Spirit," from *Forgiveness: Freed to Love*, by Christine Betz Hall, © 2023 by Pendle Hill Publications, reprinted by permission.

"If we have been swayed from the place of resting in your grace today," from *Every Moment Holy*, Vol 1, by Douglas Kaine McKelvey (Rabbit Room Press 2017), www.EveryMomentHoly.com, reprinted by permission.

"May God be with our family," prayer by Julie Palmer, © copyright www.lords-prayer-words.com. Used by permission.

"Night Prayer" and "God our Creator, our centre," from *A New Zealand Prayer Book—He Karakia Mihionare o Aotearoa*, by the Anglican Church in Aotearoa, New Zealand and Polynesia, © 1989, reprinted by permission.

"There are two things to know about forgiveness," from "Misunderstanding Forgiveness," by Janaki Spickard Keeler, *The Quietist Quaker*, © June 23, 2015, reprinted by permission.

"We have to accept that things like this do happen and will happen," from *Living in Dark Times*, by Rex Ambler, © 2017 by Pendle Hill Publications, reprinted by permission.

"What if you want to say, 'No, this [caregiving] work is not for me,'" from *A Tender Time: Quaker Voices on the End of Life*, by Patricia M. Nesbitt and Kristin Camitta Zimet, © 2024 by Baltimore Yearly Meeting of the Religious Society of Friends, reprinted by permission.

"When did I give and receive the most love today?" from *Sleeping With Bread: Holding What Gives You Life*, by Dennis Linn, Sheila Fabricant Linn, and Matthew Linn, © 1995 by Paulist Press, reprinted by permission.

Acknowledgments

Heartfelt thanks to:

First and foremost: Swarthmore Friends Meeting in Swarthmore, Pennsylvania. People from this meeting provided every kind of help that a person pregnant with a book could desire. I'm grateful for this loving community that has become my spiritual home.

Janaki Spickard Keeler for generously sharing her multitudinous kinds of expertise, including copyediting when this book was a newborn.

Eugenia Tietz-Sokolskaya for her expert help in many directions, including copyediting when this book was mature.

Joan Broadfield, for providing sanctuary while I worked on the manuscript, and for editing suggestions.

Joel Cook and Mary Hadley for meticulous and invaluable editing suggestions, proofreading, and opinion-giving at numerous stages of the manuscript.

Marcelle Martin for her unique and insightful suggestions.

Immaculate Heart of Mary Abbey, Benedictine Congregation of Solesmes, Westfield, VT, for their openness to retreats by non-Christians. My many stays there formed part of the bedrock of my spiritual life and interfaith outlook.

St. Stephen's Episcopal Church, Middlebury, VT, for inviting singers of other faiths into their Taizé choir, and for their rapid organization of online compline services when the church doors closed because of COVID-19. The "Night Service" used in those services was the stimulus for my writing this book.

Encouragement, help, or resources from: Lilith Swygert for heroic technical help with computer programs, Lake Forest Friends Meeting (IL) for providing a copy of their new *Faith and Practice* to everyone who worships there, Lynne Piersol for sending me the Hope Edelman quotation after my mother's death, Sue Edwards for a hilarious hour we spent together staging humorous author photos, Denise Williams for general support, Patricia Eldridge for her assistance with the Harriet Tubman quotation, Peter Bishop for his online Quaker Taizé worship, and Tony Martin for his wise opinions of readings.

Libraries! I'm grateful for libraries, especially those of:

- Immaculate Heart of Mary Abbey, Westfield, VT
- Philadelphia Yearly Meeting
- Pendle Hill, Wallingford, PA
- Swarthmore College (Friends Historical Library), PA
- Swarthmore Friends Meeting, PA
- Ilsley Library & interlibrary loan system, Middlebury, VT
- Swarthmore Public Library in PA, its patient Circulation Manager Carol Mackin, and its parent system, the Delaware County library system. This network of libraries has an amazing collection of non-fiction related to spirituality, including obscure books I thought I had no hope of finding.

I. Introduction

For many years, my habit has been to go to monasteries and abbeys when I need a retreat. Though not Christian, I always participate in the prayers. The nuns or monks pray in Latin and English; I join in for the prayers that I know, and pray silently the rest of the time. They are praying to God, I am praying to God—it doesn't matter to me that we say some of the same words and some different ones. Prayers from many faiths and spiritual paths speak the words of my heart or offer valuable guidance.

I especially love the compline service at 8:30 or 9:00 pm, the last worship of the day, after which the nuns or monks go to bed. Though I stay up much later, it sanctifies the evening and brings a quiet mind and a serene ending to the day. When I return home, I miss it.

In the spring of 2020, St. Stephen's Episcopal Church of Middlebury, Vermont, decided to hold six Tuesday evening compline services using chants from the Taizé community in France. They needed singers, so I signed on. For spoken prayers, they used the New Zealand Anglican Church's "Night Prayer." I loved those prayers.

They say, from the Psalms: "I will lie down in peace and take my rest, for it is in God alone that I dwell unafraid."

And:

Lord,
it is night.
The night is for stillness.
Let me be still in the presence of God.

It is night after a long day.
What has been done has been done;
what has not been done has not been done;
let it be.

The night is dark.
Let our fears of the darkness of the world
and of our own lives rest in You.[1]

I said the prayers on my own on the nights we didn't sing.

COVID-19 struck just before the third compline service. We did that one standing far apart around the perimeter of the sanctuary. By the following Tuesday, the church had closed its doors. I continued praying compline every night.

Over the next year, I expanded my choices for compline by collecting evening prayers and readings from many faiths, spiritual paths, and secular sources. I am a Quaker: a member of the Religious Society of Friends. I presented Quaker evening worship services using some of those readings, along with singing together and plenty of our beloved Quaker listening silence.

The worship also included a brief form of *examen*. Some Friends call this practice a time of collection. Before going to sleep, one reviews the day: What has gone well? What has disappointed me? Where have I fallen short? What am I feeling as a whole?

I added a look at the next day: Do I fear it? Am I worried about something? Do I need help from God or from other people to get through it? What am I feeling as a whole?

People enjoyed this form of worship and found it valuable.

One day I saw that I had put together a whole book of interfaith readings and spiritual practices. I offer it to you. I hope these prayers, thoughts, meditations, and poems will help you put the day to rest and, with God as your final thought, with your heart at ease, sleep deeply and well.

ABOUT THE TEXT

Names for God

I had to abandon the words "God" and "Lord" for a long time—they held too much baggage. To me, they meant characteristics that didn't apply to the non-gendered, loving God that I experienced. So I used "Goda" and "Lorda" (to combine masculine and feminine) until the old ideas had faded entirely from my consciousness.

Now I can say "God" or "Lord" and it brings a breeze of fresh air, and a sweet, speedy way into the dimension of the Divine. It took about four years.

A few years ago, another refreshing change came into my prayer life when I found lists of names for God used by early Quakers. They include: Kind Leader, All-sufficient Helper, Blessed Teacher, Gracious Benefactor, Holy Leaven, Never-failing Fountain, Spirit of Light and Truth, Sure Guide, and Spring of Life. It feels astonishingly different to address a prayer to the Fountain of Life, or to the Light Within Me, or to the Infinite Spirit of Love (this last one is from Evelyn Underhill).

I encourage you to do what you need to do, including changing names and words, in order to be receptive to the wisdom in this book's readings and prayers.

Translating archaic language

In addition to simply providing the readings, I have worked to make them more accessible to modern readers. Many of my favorite quotations are by early Friends. Some of the original words no longer have meaning for us. In the worst cases, words from the 17th and 18th centuries now mean the opposite of what they meant when the quotes were written.

Meaning is also affected by nearly all of the authors from those centuries, and some from more recent times, taking for granted different societal roles for women than are true today. Also, quite a few of the readings have gender bias in general and in referring to God. In my adaptations, I have changed the readings to avoid this, except for a handful of passages where I didn't feel clear to do so, such as the opening quotation from Harriet Tubman.

These difficulties are in addition to the many references to specifically Christian concepts, with which some people are not familiar now, especially our younger generations. I have provided explanations or alternate wording for these. Some words such as "truth" and "Christ" had a specific meaning to Quakers of the time that is different from what is understood today, so these also needed to be updated or elaborated.

I consulted a number of previous adaptations and commentaries, including those in *Devotional Classics*, edited by Richard Foster and James Smith, *Undaunted Zeal*, edited by Elsa F. Glines, *The Messenger That Goes Before*, by Michael Birkel, and *Truth of the Heart*, by Rex Ambler. Glines and Ambler, in particular, consulted a wealth of sources, for which I'm grateful.

In all cases, I used *lectio divina* (see p. xx) and prayer to open myself to let the meaning come. To compensate for my errors and lacks, to enable you, too, to let the meaning come, and to respect the authors, the original texts immediately follow the adaptations. Where the only adaptation of a text is changing male nouns and pronouns to neutral ones, or "man" to "people" or the like, I have not seen a need to include the original version.

After much discernment, I believe the authors would support these changes. They spoke in the language of their time; I think they would welcome us speaking their thoughts in the language of our time, as long as the original version of their words is included.

In summary

The editors of *A New Zealand Prayerbook,* in which I found the "Night Prayer," said this about updating their liturgy:

> We have gradually been compelled in our pilgrimage to start searching for ways to address God in language which is other than masculine and triumphal.

> The purpose of liturgy is not to protect particular linguistic forms. It is to enable a community to pray. We know that some people will consider we have moved too far in the language we have chosen: others will insist that we have not gone far enough . . .
>
> Even new words are only a vehicle for the worship of God, so that we might reach for the things beyond the words in the language of the heart . . .
>
> It is our hope that the use of these services will enable us to worship God in our own authentic voice . . .[2]

This says perfectly what is in my heart.

HOW TO USE THIS BOOK

Sometimes we are so tired we can only mumble a few words we know by heart before we fall asleep. Sometimes we need a couple of hours to put a difficult day to rest and be able to fall asleep. Sometimes we have a beloved prayer we want to say every night, and other times we crave something new.

The readings here are arranged so that you can turn to a new set of readings each night for forty nights. There you will find selections around a common theme, arranged like this:

- A reading or questions for reflection to settle the day (see "Why we need to settle the day," p. xxi)
- A lesson
- An intention or affirmation
- A prayer

There are many different ways you can use this book. I will suggest three.

Fully directed: Go through the book in order, using a single set of readings each night.

Semi-directed to meet specific needs of the night: Begin with the reading to settle the day. Depending upon what you find in yourself during this process, you may want to choose a different topic for the night's readings. On subsequent nights, you can continue using the pages for that topic until you feel clear or wish to move on.

For example, let's say you're going through the book in order and are on page 46, and the settling the day exercise shows you that you're full of anger. The nightly reading is about forgiving others, so you decide that, instead, you'd like to use the readings about anger. You turn to the Table of Contents to find that chapter. After working with the first set of readings on that page, if you then feel settled, you're ready for sleep.

If you don't feel settled yet, then you may need more. Read as many entries in this section as you need. The next night, if anger is still an issue, continue with that section. If this is an important subject for you, you may need to repeat these readings for many nights. You may want to read some of them during the day, too.

When anger isn't an issue any longer, or you have gone as far as you can with it for the time being, go back to page 46, where you were before you began to work with anger.

Self-directed: Do one of the settling the day readings first every night. There are three of these, each of which is repeated for ten nights. New ones begin on page 3, 32, and 59. Then on page 86, the style changes to a quotation followed by questions. Each of these sets is repeated for two nights.

After settling the day, use any combination of the following methods or invent your own:

- Open the book randomly and see what you get.
- Use the First line, Title and Key Phrase Index or the General Index at the back of the book to choose what appeals to you.
- Work through the various subjects in the Table of Contents one by one in the order of your choice.

Sacred reading

I recommend that you read in a *lectio divina* (sacred reading) style: read very slowly, pausing between phrases, and out loud if you can. If phrases are dense with meaning, don't go on. Instead, repeat a phrase several times to give yourself a chance to fully absorb it. Wait for a minute or more in between readings to let the words reverberate. If it's a brief reading, repeat the entire reading this way at least three times.

Lectio divina is the opposite of analytical reading. It is not intellectual; it's aimed at the heart. This method is designed to cause a reading to sink into you deeply, and to help your heart open to understand it on multiple levels. The goal is for the words to bring you closer to God.

Why we need to settle the day

The practice of *examen* (Latin for "examine") comes to us from the Jesuit monastic tradition of the 1600s. It is a technique of prayerful reflection on the events of the day. In this book, I have adapted it for lay people and call it "settling the day."

We ask ourselves questions such as, When was I my best self today? Did I see that of God in others? Were there any times I could have done better? Do I feel overwhelmed by what tomorrow holds? What can I do about that?

In this book, I add a gratitude practice if it's not embedded in the reading.

We do this practice to make peace with our day, ourselves, each other, and God. This reduces stress, helps us sleep well, and helps us cope better with whatever tomorrow brings.

The process of settling helps us to be real about what we are feeling and how our lives are going, so we realize the truth of things instead of denying it.

It helps us recognize our failings so we can try to become better people. Over time, we see our progress as well as our shortcomings.

Through it, we grow a practice of thanksgiving, giving ourselves "lift" to soar despite life's vicissitudes.

Settling practices can develop intimacy within the family if we do it with our spouses or partners, or do a simple form nightly with our children.

If you find it hard to do on your own, you can do it on a weekly or monthly basis with a friend, a small group of friends, or a faithfulness group.

If you like, before asking yourself the settling questions, add to the ritual by lighting a candle, sitting in a special place or in front of an altar, or having a time of silence, meditation, or worship. Some people add journaling, drawing, or settle the day while outside in nature.

Besides an ongoing settling practice, I recommend doing an extended version annually. Ask yourself the same basic questions about the past year, instead of the past day. It is essential to know how you feel about things, and to be honest with yourself about how your life is going. It is essential to know if you are accumulating frustrations, sorrows, resentments, or anger. On the other hand, you may be overwhelmed by present problems and have forgotten how far you've actually come this year, how good a year it's really been. Taking stock through this series of questions can restore your larger perspective and enthusiasm for meeting challenges.

I recommend that once you have tried all of the versions of settling in this book, you choose one that works for you and stay with that form, at least for a while. That way, your heart will learn it and it will become habitual. If at some point it becomes lifeless, then choose another version or design your own.

With young children, especially, you should stay with the same form so it becomes second nature for them. When they become mature enough to deepen or broaden their exploration, then it's time for a change.

ENDNOTES

1. Anglican Church in Aotearoa, "Night Prayer," *New Zealand Prayer Book*, 183.
2. Anglican Church in Aotearoa, *New Zealand Prayer Book*, xii–xiv.

Come and take your seat in the bosom of the limitless.
At sunrise open and raise your heart
like a blossoming flower
and at sunset bend your head
and in silence complete the worship
of the day.
—Rabindranath Tagore

II. Nightly Readings

Help and hope

SETTLING THE DAY

Consider:

- What happened today for which you have gratitude?
- What happened today that you will do better or differently next time?
    - The idea is to make peace with your day and with yourself.
    - Take some time to do this. Then when you're ready to go on:
- What qualities will you need for tomorrow? (For example: forgiveness, fortitude, patience.)
    - Find these in yourself or pray for whatever you will need.
    - The idea is to let go of concern about tomorrow, to be at peace.

Take some time to do this. Then when you're ready, go on to the Lesson.

LESSON

'Twant me, 'twas the Lord. I always told Him, "I trust to you. I don't know where to go or what to do, but I expect You to lead me," and He always did.[1]
—Harriet Tubman

AFFIRMATION & INTENTION

In peace I will both lie down and sleep, for it is in God alone that I dwell unafraid.[2]
—The Psalms

PRAYER

On many an idle day
have I grieved over lost time.
But it is never lost, my Lord.
Thou hast taken every moment of
my life in Thine own hands.

Hidden in the heart of things
Thou art nourishing seeds into sprouts,
buds into blossoms,
and ripening flowers into fruitfulness.

I was tired and sleeping on my idle bed
and imagined all work had ceased.
In the morning I woke up and found
my garden full with wonders of flowers.[3]
—Rabindranath Tagore

SETTLING THE DAY

Consider:

- What happened today for which you have gratitude?
- What happened today that you will do better or differently next time?
    - The idea is to make peace with your day and with yourself.
    - Take some time to do this. Then when you're ready to go on:
- What qualities will you need for tomorrow? (For example: forgiveness, fortitude, patience.)
    - Find these in yourself or pray for whatever you will need.
    - The idea is to let go of concern about tomorrow, to be at peace.

Take some time to do this. Then when you're ready, go on to the Lesson.

LESSON

God carries me and brings me to mount up as on eagles' wings, over all their storms, and waves, and floods that they cast out against me.[4]
—George Fox, 1656

AFFIRMATION & INTENTION

May I know you more clearly
love you more dearly
follow you more nearly
day by day.[5]
—St. Richard, Bishop of Chichester, 1253

PRAYER

Evening Prayer

Before the end of daylight we beseech You,
Creator of the world
that out of Your customary tenderness,
You may be the protector Who guards us.

May our hearts dream of You,
may they experience You during sleep,

and may they always sing Your glory
as the light returns.[6]
—Christian prayer

SETTLING THE DAY

Consider:

- What happened today for which you have gratitude?
- What happened today that you will do better or differently next time?
    - The idea is to make peace with your day and with yourself.
    - Take some time to do this. Then when you're ready to go on:
- What qualities will you need for tomorrow? (For example: forgiveness, fortitude, patience.)
    - Find these in yourself or pray for whatever you will need.
    - The idea is to let go of concern about tomorrow, to be at peace.

Take some time to do this. Then when you're ready, go on to the Lesson.

LESSON

Are there times when you are in distress but it doesn't occur to you to ask Spirit for help?

Do you feel you don't deserve to receive divine help?

Do you feel you are supposed to be strong, able, and invincible, so should ask for help only if circumstances are dire?

It is not childish or dependent or weak to ask for help when you need it. Love delights in giving.

—Shulamith Clearbridge

AFFIRMATION & INTENTION

May the words of my mouth be accepted,
and the murmurs of my heart,
as I face you, God, my rock, my redeemer![7]
—The Psalms

PRAYER

As we bring these gifts before you, gracious God, we ask that you continue to ask much of us, expect much from us, enable much by us, encourage many through us. Amen.[8]
—Sarah Reynolds

I like to say it like this:

Gracious, generous God, I am grateful.
Ask much of me.
Expect much of me.
I pray you can enable much through me.
Amen.

SETTLING THE DAY

Consider:

- What happened today for which you have gratitude?
- What happened today that you will do better or differently next time?
    - The idea is to make peace with your day and with yourself.
    - Take some time to do this. Then when you're ready to go on:
- What qualities will you need for tomorrow? (For example: forgiveness, fortitude, patience.)
    - Find these in yourself or pray for whatever you will need.
    - The idea is to let go of concern about tomorrow, to be at peace.

Take some time to do this. Then when you're ready, go on to the Lesson.

LESSON

The winter tree
Resembles me,
Whose sap lies in its root.
The spring draws nigh;
As it, so I
Shall bud, I hope, and shoot.[9]
—Thomas Ellwood, 1639–1714

AFFIRMATION & INTENTION

Joy does not simply happen to us. We have to choose joy and keep choosing it every day. It is a choice based on the knowledge that we belong to God and have found in God our refuge and our safety and that nothing, not even death, can take God away from us.[10]
—Henri Nouwen

PRAYER

I am God's by day, I am God's by night.
Into God's hands I commit my spirit.

May my eyes behold You,
my heart feel Your joy,
and my soul know You.[11]
—Jewish prayer

ADDITIONAL READINGS ABOUT HELP AND HOPE

Adaptation:

Take heed, dear Friends, to the promptings of love and truth in your hearts. Trust that these come from God, whose light shows us our failings and brings us to new life.

—George Fox, 1694 or 1695

Original:

Take heed, dear Friends, to the promptings of love and truth in your hearts. Trust them as the leadings of God, whose light shows us our darkness and brings us to new life.[12]

The kind of hope I often think about (especially in situations that are particularly hopeless, such as prison) I understand above all as a state of mind, not a state of the world. Either we have hope within us or we don't; it is a dimension of the soul; it's not essentially dependent on some particular observation of the world or estimate of the situation. Hope is not prognostication. It is an orientation of the spirit, an orientation of the heart; it transcends the world that is immediately experienced, and is anchored somewhere beyond its horizons.[13]

—Vaclav Havel

We will plant songs where there were curses.[14]

—Joy Harjo

With all my heart I have sought You;
please help me not to wander from Your path.

Your word I have treasured in my heart,

Your testimonies also are my delight;
they are my counselors.

When my soul cleaves to the dust;
I know You will revive me.

My soul weeps because of grief;
you anchor me and give me strength.

You enlarge my heart.

You have made me hope.

Your statutes are my songs
in the house of my pilgrimage.

The earth is full of Your lovingkindness, O Lord.

You have revived me with Your lovingkindness.

Your faithfulness continues to all generations.

I am Yours.

Your word is a lamp to my feet
and a light to my path.

You are my shield;
I rely on You.

My eyes anticipate the night watches,
that I may meditate on You.

You are near, O Lord,
and Your love is the Truth.

I long for You, O Lord.
You save me,
and Your Truth is my delight.[15]
—The Psalms

Fear and worry

SETTLING THE DAY

Consider:

- What happened today for which you have gratitude?
- What happened today that you will do better or differently next time?
    - The idea is to make peace with your day and with yourself.
    - Take some time to do this. Then when you're ready to go on:
- What qualities will you need for tomorrow? (For example: forgiveness, fortitude, patience.)
    - Find these in yourself or pray for whatever you will need.
    - The idea is to let go of concern about tomorrow, to be at peace.

Take some time to do this. Then when you're ready, go on to the Lesson.

LESSON

Adaptation:

Friends, there is no blockage in the Fountain of Life. Oh the fullness, oh the depth, height, breadth and length of God's love! How God has helped in the hour of distress, conquering and scattering the enemies which the heart was often ready to say were unconquerable! How the Lord has put an end to the doubts, fears, disputes, and troubles with which the mind was overwhelmed and tossed! And now God extends peace like a river; now the Lord brings the soul out of the desert into a green and welcoming land, now it is satisfied and delighted!

It is the day of the working of the Lord's tender hand! May the Spirit of Light and Truth remove that which stands in your way. And if you wait faithfully, and serve that Spirit, you will grow in truth and power.

Friends, are you troubled by thoughts, fears, doubts, imaginations, reasonings, etc.? Oh do not fear them! Do not look at them and become discouraged by them; rather look to the Lord! Look up to the power which defeats all their strength. Wait for the descending of that power upon you. Abide in the faith of divine help; wait in patience until the Lord acts.

Do not let your troubles stir you up, though they fill your soul, for there is something into which they cannot enter, and from which patience, faith and hope will spring up in you, no matter what is happening outwardly.

Now, Friends, in your daily struggles, if you attentively serve God, and surrender your will, the weak and fearful parts of you will die away. And you will receive from God that which will help, relieve, refresh and satisfy you.

And then, as to what may befall us outwardly in these hard times, shall we not trust our tender Lord and rest satisfied? Yes, the Lord can bear up our mind and be our strength, armor, rock, peace, joy and full satisfaction in every condition. For it is not the condition that makes us miserable, but the lack of God in the condition. Let us not then be like the worldly and judge or fear according to the appearance of things. Rather, let us enshrine the Lord of hosts in our hearts, and this shall be a sanctuary for us in the storms and tempests which are coming down heavily upon the world.

Thus, my dear friends, let us let go of our worries and dwell in the peace which God breathes. Let us rest in patience, with a quiet heart, night and day, which nothing can wear out or disturb.

May God, with tender mercy, guide our hearts daily more and more into this way of living, until we abide here fully and always.

—Isaac Penington, written while in prison, 1667

Original:

Friends, there is no straitness in the Fountain of Life. . . . oh the fulness, oh the depth, height, breadth, and length of the love! . . . how hath He helped in the hour of distress! How hath he conquered and scattered the enemies! which, in the unbelief, the heart was ready often to say, were unconquerable . . . How hath He put an end to doubts, fears, disputes, troubles, wherewith the mind was overwhelmed and tossed! and now He extends peace like a river; now He puts the soul forth out of the pit, into the green pastures; now it feeds on the freshness of life, and . . . is delighted! . . .

It is the day of love, of mercy, of kindness, of the working of the tender hand; of the wisdom, power, and goodness of our God, manifested richly in Jesus Christ!

. . . The Lord remove that which stands in the way; and, in the faithful waiting on the power which is arisen . . . growth in His truth and power is witnessed by those that wait upon him.

May the Lord God, in His tender mercy . . . guide our hearts daily more and more in the travel, and into the possession of this . . . and may also daily, further and further, travel into what is yet before.

Friends . . . Are ye troubled with thoughts, fears, doubts, imaginations, reasonings, etc.? Oh! do not fear it; do not look at it, so as to be discouraged by it; but look to Him! Look up to the power which is over all their strength; wait for the descendings of the power upon you; abide in faith of the Lord's help, and wait in patience till the Lord arise. . . . So be still before Him, and, in stillness, believe in His name; yea, enter not into the hurryings of the enemy, though they fill the soul; for there is yet somewhat to which they cannot enter, from whence patience, faith, and hope will spring up in you, even in the midst of all that they can do.

Now, Friends, in a sensible waiting and giving up to the Lord, in the daily exercise, by the daily cross to that in you which is not of the life, this work will daily go on; and ye will feel from the Lord, that which will help, relieve, refresh, and satisfy. . . . And then, as to what may befall us outwardly, in this confused state of things, shall we not trust our tender Father, and rest satisfied in His will? . . . shall He not bear up the mind, and be our strength, portion, armor, rock, peace, joy, and full satisfaction in every condition? For it is not the condition makes miserable, but the want of Him in the condition. . . . Let us then not look out like the world, or judge or fear according to the appearance of things, after the manner of the world; but let us sanctify the Lord of hosts in our hearts . . . and He shall be an hiding place unto us in the storms, and in the tempests, which are coming thick upon the earth.

Thus, my dear friends, let us retire, and dwell in the peace which God breathes, and lie down in the Lamb's patience and stillness, night and day, which nothing can wear out or disturb.[16]

AFFIRMATION & INTENTION

[Let me be] . . . tranquil . . . in . . . trust listening ever to Eternity's whisper, walking with a smile into the dark.[17]
—Thomas R. Kelly

PRAYER

Lord,
it is night.
The night is for stillness.
Let me be still in the presence of God.

It is night after a long day.
What has been done has been done;
what has not been done has not been done;
let it be.

The night is dark.
Let my fears of the darkness of the world
and of my own life rest in You.

The night is quiet.
Let the quietness of Your peace enfold me,
all dear to me
and all who have no peace.

The night heralds the dawn.
Let me look expectantly to a new day,
new joys,
new possibilities.

Amen.[18]
—The Anglican Church in Aotearoa,
New Zealand and Polynesia

SETTLING THE DAY

Consider:

- What happened today for which you have gratitude?
- What happened today that you will do better or differently next time?
  - The idea is to make peace with your day and with yourself.
  - Take some time to do this. Then when you're ready to go on:
- What qualities will you need for tomorrow? (For example: forgiveness, fortitude, patience.)
  - Find these in yourself or pray for whatever you will need.
  - The idea is to let go of concern about tomorrow, to be at peace.

Take some time to do this. Then when you're ready, go on to the Lesson.

LESSON

In the monastic tradition, the highest form of sanctity is to live in hell and not lose hope. [This boy] clings to his hope and his faith and his GED certificate and chooses to march, resilient, into his future.[19]

—Gregory Boyle

AFFIRMATION & INTENTION

Adaptation:

In all things, drink in the divine power from above, whereby you may become mightily strengthened. Sink down into God. Here you will be protected from above, and can look for God to overcome all things.[20]

—James Nayler, 1618–1660

Original:

. . . and so in all things with desire, drinking in of the heavenly virtue from above, whereby you may become strengthened with all might . . . which is done by sinking down into the heavenly feeling, whereby you will be overshadowed from above, from whence the savior is looked for, to overcome things below.

PRAYER

Adaptation:

It is in my heart to praise You, O my God;
let me never forget what you have been to me in the night by Your presence.

In the day of trial when I was beset in darkness,
when I was assaulted with strong temptations,
then Your presence in secret did preserve me.

When the floods sought to sweep me away,
You encompassed them.
When my way was through the sea,
and when I passed under the mountains,
You were present with me.

When the weight of the hills was upon me, You upheld me;
otherwise I would have sunk under the earth.

When I was altogether helpless
when I was full of anger and passed by the gates of hell
when I was between the millstones,
and as one crushed with the weight of his enemy,
as a father You were with me.

You answered me, saying,
I will set you above all your fears,
and lift up your feet above what oppresses you.

I believed and was strengthened, and Your word saved me.
Glory, glory to You, sings my soul,
and let my heart be ever filled with thanksgiving
because You lifted me out of the pit.[21]
—James Nayler

Original:

It is in my heart to praise thee, O my God; let me never forget thee what thou hast been to me in the night by thy presence, in the day of trial when I was beset in darkness . . . and when I was assaulted with strong temptations, then thy presence in secret did preserve me. . . . When the floods sought to sweep me away, thou settest a compass for them . . . when my way was through the sea, and when I passed under the mountains, there wert thou present with me, when the weight of the hills was upon me thou upheldst me, else had I sunk under the earth; when I was as one altogether helpless . . . when I went on the way of wrath and passed by the gates of hell . . . when I was between the millstones, and as one crushed with the weight of his adversary: as a father thou wert with me . . . thou answeredst me . . . saying, I will set thee above all thy fears, and lift up thy feet above the head of oppression. I believed and was strengthened, and thy word was salvation. . . . Glory, glory to thee, saith my soul, and let my heart be ever filled with thanksgiving . . . then didst thou lift me out of the pit.

SETTLING THE DAY

Consider:

- What happened today for which you have gratitude?
- What happened today that you will do better or differently next time?
    - The idea is to make peace with your day and with yourself.
    - Take some time to do this. Then when you're ready to go on:
- What qualities will you need for tomorrow? (For example: forgiveness, fortitude, patience.)
    - Find these in yourself or pray for whatever you will need.
    - The idea is to let go of concern about tomorrow, to be at peace.

Take some time to do this. Then when you're ready, go on to the Lesson.

LESSON

Adaptation:

And though the waves and storms be high, yet your faith will enable you to swim above them, for they are but for a time, and the Truth is outside time. And do not think that anything will outlast the Truth. It stands firm and is victorious over that which is not the Truth; for the good will overcome the evil; and the light, darkness, and the life, death; and virtue, vice; and righteousness, unrighteousness. So be faithful, and live in that state of mind which exists outside of time.

—George Fox, 1671

Original:

And though the waves and storms be high, yet your faith will keep you to swim above them, for they are but for a time, and the Truth is without time. . . . And do not think that anything will outlast the Truth, which standeth sure and is over that which is out of the Truth; for the good will overcome the evil; and the light, darkness, and the life, death; and virtue, vice; and righteousness, unrighteousness. The false prophet cannot overcome the true, but the true prophet, Christ, will overcome all the false. So be faithful, and live in that which doth not think the time long . . .[22]

AFFIRMATION & INTENTION

The body fears.
The soul soars!
Search for the part of you that knows no fear.
Try to live *there*[23]
—Shulamith Clearbridge

PRAYER

[God], sink into me like water into parched ground.
I am in need of Your life-giving sweetness.
Cleansing Spirit, fall upon me like rain onto a dusty city.
I am in need of your purifying [waters].[24]
—Mary van Balen Holt

SETTLING THE DAY

Consider:

- What happened today for which you have gratitude?
- What happened today that you will do better or differently next time?
    - The idea is to make peace with your day and with yourself.
    - Take some time to do this. Then when you're ready to go on:

- What qualities will you need for tomorrow? (For example: forgiveness, fortitude, patience.)
    - Find these in yourself or pray for whatever you will need.
    - The idea is to let go of concern about tomorrow, to be at peace.

Take some time to do this. Then when you're ready, go on to the Lesson.

LESSON

It is but lost labor that we haste to rise up early,
and so late take rest,
and eat the bread of anxiety.
For those beloved of God are
given gifts even while they sleep.[25]
—THE PSALMS

AFFIRMATION & INTENTION

Once there was a Buddhist farmer whose horse ran away. That evening, all of his neighbors came over to commiserate. They said, "We are so sorry to hear your horse has run away. This is most unfortunate." The farmer said, "Maybe."

A few days later, the horse came back bringing seven wild horses with it. Everybody came back and said, "Oh, isn't that lucky! What a great turn of events. You now have eight horses!" The farmer answered, "Maybe."

The following day his son tried to ride one of the horses. He was thrown off and broke his leg. The neighbors then said, "Oh dear, that's too bad," and the farmer responded, "Maybe."

Two weeks later, army officers came to the neighborhood to draft people into the army. They rejected the farmer's son because he had a broken leg. Again all the neighbors came around saying, "Isn't that great!" The farmer replied, "Maybe."[26]

—Buddhist or Taoist story

I will not worry yet. I will wait to see what happens next. I will let a long view keep me calm.

PRAYER

Dear God, I surrender everything to You—my fear, my need for control, my emotions. There are times when I choose fear over faith, and I'm ready to change my ways. Keep me close to You, and when You see that I'm falling off course, please give me strength. In Your holy name, I pray. Amen.[27]

—Christian prayer

SETTLING THE DAY

Consider:

- What happened today for which you have gratitude?
- What happened today that you will do better or differently next time?
    - The idea is to make peace with your day and with yourself.
    - Take some time to do this. Then when you're ready to go on:
- What qualities will you need for tomorrow? (For example: forgiveness, fortitude, patience.)
    - Find these in yourself or pray for whatever you will need.
    - The idea is to let go of concern about tomorrow, to be at peace.

Take some time to do this. Then when you're ready, go on to the Lesson.

LESSON

Fear can sometimes be a good thing. We discover what is important to us, who is important to us. We discover what we are capable of and what we are not—who we are, in fact. Our priorities straighten out as everything is stripped away except what is essential. The dross and dress fall away. We meet something, and fear it, and come out the other side emptied, plain, with a great emptiness in our minds and lives which we can fill with worship.[28]
—Shulamith Clearbridge

AFFIRMATION & INTENTION

There are blessings even in my fears. I will find them.
—Shulamith Clearbridge

PRAYER

O Source of life and strength, you are the strong hold of my life.
So why should I fear?
I yearn to dwell in Your house constantly,
to feel the joy of visiting Your sanctuary.
In a day of trouble, I will enter Your abode;
You will shelter me; You will lift me upon a rock.

I will bring offerings of jubilation;
I will sing songs of joy to You.
Divine and all-bountiful Hand, please hear me.
Please answer me.
My heart said, "Seek God," and I have done so ever since.
You have ever been my help.
Even if my mother and my father leave me,
You are with me.
Please show me Your ways. Lead me in Your right path.

I place my hope in God.
I will be strong and let my heart take courage.[29]
—The Psalms

ADDITIONAL READINGS ABOUT FEAR AND WORRY

And so our Good Lord answered to all the questions and doubts which I could raise, saying most comfortingly: I may make all things well, and I can make all things well, and I shall make all things well . . . And you will see yourself that every kind of thing will be well . . . And in these . . . words, God wishes us to be enclosed in rest and in peace.[30]
—Julian of Norwich, 1342–1419

What has happened to you is happening in a greater or less [*sic*] degree to everyone. The present abnormal conditions are as bad for the spiritual life as for every other kind of life. We are all finding it frightfully difficult and most of us are failing badly. The material world and its interests, uproars and perplexities are so insistent . . . All the same of course it is essential to hold on as well as you can and make a resolute and regular act of willed attention to God at the times set apart for prayer—only do not fuss at the poor and unappetizing results. The will is what matters . . .[31]
—Evelyn Underhill

If we can abide peacefully in the ultimate dimension, we will not drown in the ocean of suffering, grief, fear and despair.[32]
—Thích Nhất Hạnh

Courage is resistance to fear, mastery of fear—not absence of fear.[33]
—Mark Twain

Quiet minds cannot be perplexed or frightened, but go on in fortune or misfortune at their own private pace, like a clock during a thunderstorm.[34]
—Robert Louis Stevenson

Adaptation:

Sing and rejoice, you Children of the Light, for God is at work in this thick night of darkness. We know this because Truth flourishes like a rose, and lilies grow among life's thorns, and plants grow on the hills, and gentleness, innocence and joy are there. So never heed the tempests or the storms, the floods or the rains, for the light of God is in every human being, and it triumphs over everything else. And so, be of good faith and valiant for the Truth.

—George Fox, 1663

Original:

Sing and rejoice, ye Children of the Day and of the Light, for the Lord is at work in this thick night of Darkness that may be felt: Truth doth flourish as the rose, and the lilies do grow among the thorns, and the plants atop of the hills, and upon them the lambs doth skip and play. And never heed the tempests nor the storms, floods nor rains, for the Seed Christ is over all and doth reign. And so, be of good faith and valiant for the Truth.[35]

The soul is greater than anything you ever lost.[36]

—Bahauddin

Every moment of fear is a lost moment of imagining something new.[37]

—Jane Smiley

Forgiving oneself

SETTLING THE DAY

Consider:

- What happened today for which you have gratitude?
- What happened today that you will do better or differently next time?
    - The idea is to make peace with your day and with yourself.
    - Take some time to do this. Then when you're ready to go on:
- What qualities will you need for tomorrow? (For example: forgiveness, fortitude, patience.)
    - Find these in yourself or pray for whatever you will need.
    - The idea is to let go of concern about tomorrow, to be at peace

Take some time to do this. Then when you're ready, go on to the Lesson.

LESSON

God doesn't ask that we succeed in everything, but that we are faithful.[38]
—Mother Teresa

AFFIRMATION & INTENTION

Expect mistakes.
Respect mistakes.
Learn from mistakes.[39]
—Author unknown

PRAYER

Great Spirit Prayer

Oh, Great Spirit Whose voice I hear in the winds,
And Whose breath gives life to all the world,
Hear me! I am small and weak, I need your strength and wisdom.
Let me walk in beauty,
and make my eyes ever behold the red purple sunset.
Make my hands respect the things you have made
and my ears sharp to hear your voice.
Make me wise so that I may understand the things
You have taught my people.
Let me learn the lessons You have hidden in every leaf and rock.
I seek strength not to be greater than any other,
but to fight my greatest enemy, myself.
Make me always ready to come to You with clean hands
and straight eyes,
so when life fades, as the fading sunset,
my spirit may come to You without shame.[40]
—Lakota prayer

SETTLING THE DAY

Ask yourself:

When did I give and receive the most love today?
When did I give and receive the least love today?

When did I feel most alive today?
When did I most feel life draining out of me?

When today did I have the greatest sense of belonging to myself, others, God and the universe?
When did I have the least sense of belonging?

When was I happiest today?
When was I saddest?

What was today's high point?
What was today's low point?
—DENNIS LINN, SHEILA FABRICANT LINN, MATTHEW LINN

LESSON

We all betray ourselves and other people, at least in some measure, at times in our lives. To be loyal and to betray are human characteristics that are not the exclusive province of saints or traitors. Life is tough and sometimes fear is too great to uphold ideals that we can sustain and invoke during easier times.[41]
—THEODORE I. RUBIN, MD

AFFIRMATION & INTENTION

To a child a few weeks seem long. To a youth a few months seem long. To an adult a few years seem long.

To an old person decades seem short. The old person is closest to God. To God decades are seconds, centuries minutes. To God eternity is every moment.

Be patient with yourself; think like God.[42]

—Robert Van de Weyer

PRAYER

I found god in myself
& I loved her
I loved her fiercely[43]
—Ntozake Shange

SETTLING THE DAY

Ask yourself:

When did I give and receive the most love today?
When did I give and receive the least love today?

When did I feel most alive today?
When did I most feel life draining out of me?

When today did I have the greatest sense of belonging to myself, others, God and the universe?
When did I have the least sense of belonging?

When was I happiest today?
When was I saddest?

What was today's high point?
What was today's low point?
—DENNIS LINN, SHEILA FABRICANT LINN, MATTHEW LINN

LESSON

An act of love that fails is just as much a part of the divine life as an act of love that succeeds. For love is measured by its fullness and not by its reception.[44]
—HAROLD LOUKES

AFFIRMATION & INTENTION

I feel like writing you a rather bracing, disagreeable, east-windy sort of letter. When I read yours my first impulse was to send you a line begging you only to let yourself alone. Don't keep on pulling yourself to pieces . . . It is emphatically your business now to look forwards and not backwards: and also to look forwards in an eager and optimistic spirit. Any other course is mere ingratitude, you know . . .

Our Lord did not say, "Come unto me all ye faultless": neither were we told, "Be sure you tear yourselves to pieces first . . . "

There. God bless you.[45]

—Evelyn Underhill

I will forgive myself for not being perfect.

PRAYER

. . . and in those situations where my strength or skill is not enough to aid or save, when loss or harm proves irreparable, let me neither rage against you nor against my own limits, O Lord, but let me instead find humility to trust your sovereignty, and to comfort others however I can.[46]

—Douglas McKelvey

SETTLING THE DAY

Ask yourself:

When did I give and receive the most love today?
When did I give and receive the least love today?

When did I feel most alive today?
When did I most feel life draining out of me?

When today did I have the greatest sense of belonging to myself, others, God and the universe?
When did I have the least sense of belonging?

When was I happiest today?
When was I saddest?

What was today's high point?
What was today's low point?
—Dennis Linn, Sheila Fabricant Linn, Matthew Linn

LESSON

Adaptation:
Serve God diligently and attentively,
letting that part of you which is pure lead the way.

Though you see little
and know little
and have little,

and see your emptiness
and your limitations
and how little you have accomplished,

and see the hardness of your heart
and your own unworthiness,

it is the light of Spirit that reveals all this,
and it is a sign of God's love of you
that it is shown to you.
—George Fox, 1652

Original:

Wait upon God in that which is pure. Though you see little, and know little, and have little, and see your emptiness, and see your nakedness, and barrenness, and unfruitfulness, and see the hardness of your hearts, and your own unworthiness; it is the light that discovers all this, and the love of God to you.[47]

AFFIRMATION & INTENTION

. . . befriending my mistakes . . .
. . . lay my hand where my heart aches . . .[48]
—Carrie Newcomer

I befriend my mistakes. I lay my hand where my heart aches, and feel compassion for myself.

PRAYER

If we have been swayed from the place of resting in your grace today—
swayed by shame, by error, by vanity,
by pride, or by love of the praise of people,
act, O Holy Spirit!
Reveal our error, convict conscience,
and bring us to quick repentance . . .
Shape our thoughts O Lord, by your truth,
even as you shape our hearts by your love.[49]
—Douglas McKelvey

I recommend that you make this one personal: "If I have been swayed from the place of resting in your grace today . . . "

ADDITIONAL READINGS ABOUT FORGIVING ONESELF

Each of us is responsible for our own actions and our own reactions. We are not responsible for someone else's actions and reactions. This is very important for women especially because most women have been taught that they are responsible for the happiness of everyone in their family. They are taught that all family unhappiness and discord is their fault. But responsibility rests within each individual.[50]
—Alice Wiser

People should not feel bad if others are angry with them, but only if they merited the anger.[51]
—Meister Eckhart, c. 1260–1328

Failure is the key to success; each mistake teaches us something.[52]
—Morihei Ueshiba

[A doctor was caring for a patient, but had to leave temporarily. A nurse took over the care and the patient nearly died before the doctor could get back. The nurse feels responsible but the doctor thinks it was his responsibility and he shouldn't have left.]

[Nurse] "But I was responsible for her while you were gone."

[Doctor] "And you did every blasted thing you could for her. I couldn't have done any more. We knew this was risky. If Anna dies, part of me is going to hate myself till the day I die. But part of me is going to know the risk was accepted with informed consent, and we did the best we could."

[The nurse] shook her head, seeking some reassurance . . . "How can you not wonder if there was something else we should have done, something we didn't think of?"

[The doctor's] blue eyes didn't flinch. "You can't."[53]

—Howard Weinstein

Tell me, friend, how can I renounce Maya*? . . .
So, when I give up passion, I see that anger remains;
And when I renounce anger, greed is with me still;
And when greed is vanquished, pride and vainglory remain;
When the mind is detached and casts Maya away,
Still it clings to the letter.

Kabir says, "Listen to me, dear friend!
The true path is rarely found."[54]
—KABIR, 1440–1518

*Maya: a Sanskrit word meaning the world we perceive with our usual senses. It also means trickery, fraud. In this context, it refers to illusion or unreality, in that we are being tricked from seeing the reality of God and our own true nature.

It is not necessary to "want God and want nothing else." You have only to "want to want God and want to want nothing else." Few get beyond this really.[55]

And:

Pray as you can, don't try to pray as you can't.[56]
—DOM JOHN CHAPMAN

What if you want to say, "No, this [caregiving] work is not for me"? You might feel inadequate, or squeezed by other responsibilities, or burned out from other caregiving. You might be exhausted and need a break. Saying no does not have to mean that you are abandoning someone. Guilt need not to be a part of asserting healthy boundaries. . . .

Above all, can you allow yourself to be good enough but not perfect? Can you commit to try your hardest, knowing you will make mistakes? You will certainly have a meltdown sometime along the way. Only agree to be Love's imperfect instrument.[57]

—PATRICIA M. NESBITT AND KRISTIN CAMITTA ZIMET

I would prefer a thousand mistakes in extravagance of love to any paralysis in wariness of fear. Our world has known too much of fear, defensiveness, and mistrust; I think we could use a healthy dose of unmitigated, mistake-making loving.[58]
—Gerald G. May

Forgiving others

SETTLING THE DAY

Ask yourself:

When did I give and receive the most love today?
When did I give and receive the least love today?

When did I feel most alive today?
When did I most feel life draining out of me?

When today did I have the greatest sense of belonging to myself, others, God and the universe?
When did I have the least sense of belonging?

When was I happiest today?
When was I saddest?

What was today's high point?
What was today's low point?
—Dennis Linn, Sheila Fabricant Linn, Matthew Linn

LESSON

Who said that forgiveness is giving up all hope of having had a different past?[59]
—Anne Lamott

AFFIRMATION & INTENTION

Forgiveness is never going to be easy. Each day it must be prayed for and struggled for and won.[60]
—Sister Helen Prejean

PRAYER

Prayers for Healing

Beloved God of Joy
I pray
I pray not to become ill.
I pray that this stress does not damage my body.
Please bring any emotions that might become seeds of illness
to the surface
where I can see and meet them.

Divine Giver of Peace
I pray to be healed of my fear
I pray to be healed of my rage
and of the constant feeling of injustice.
Even righteous rage
is not worth it if it destroys my body.

Ocean of Mercy
I want to forgive,
teach me to forgive endlessly,
help me to forgive.[61]
—Shulamith Clearbridge

SETTLING THE DAY

Ask yourself:

When did I give and receive the most love today?
When did I give and receive the least love today?

When did I feel most alive today?
When did I most feel life draining out of me?

When today did I have the greatest sense of belonging to myself, others, God and the universe?
When did I have the least sense of belonging?

When was I happiest today?
When was I saddest?

What was today's high point?
What was today's low point?
—Dennis Linn, Sheila Fabricant Linn, Matthew Linn

LESSON

There are two things to know about forgiveness. 1) It doesn't change anything. 2) It changes everything . . .

. . . [The forgiveness] was not serene or merciful on my part. I bear no resemblance to Mother Teresa . . .

In the middle of that storm of rage and grief, a choice opened up before me. I could hold onto this bitter black violence that was already rending my soul, or I could let it go. If I held onto it, I could see it would eat me alive. It would destroy me . . .

It was also a choice about the kind of world I wanted to believe in. You see, you can believe that people are evil, or you can believe that people are fundamentally good, but they do extremely evil things . . . For me, it was an act of faith to choose the latter . . . I'm a social worker; I know the evils that people are capable of committing. But I can decide that the person who commits evil is evil, or I can have faith that they too are a child of God and respond accordingly . . .

Forgiveness is a choice to see the humanity in the other person and respond to that, rather than to the evil they perpetrated . . .

Forgiveness was my way of transforming an atrocity, of not letting the person who set out to hurt [us] "win" by poisoning my soul. It was a refusal to let him have the power to shake my faith in the goodness of humanity.

Forgiveness doesn't take the pain away . . . But sometimes I think how much more painful it would have been if we hadn't been able to forgive, if we had held onto that pain and rage and let it eat us up . . .

. . . Forgiveness is something that is offered freely and has very little to do with the perpetrator. It transforms the person who does the forgiving, and gives them back some of the power that [was taken] from them.[62]

—Janaki Spickard Keeler

AFFIRMATION & INTENTION

. . . all such spirits I laid before God and left them for God to deal with.[63]

—George Fox, 1654

PRAYER

O God, scatterer of ignorance and darkness, grant me your strength. May all beings regard me with the eye of a friend, and I all beings! With the eye of a friend may each single being regard all others![64]

—Hindu Veda

SETTLING THE DAY

Ask yourself:

When did I give and receive the most love today?
When did I give and receive the least love today?

When did I feel most alive today?
When did I most feel life draining out of me?

When today did I have the greatest sense of belonging to myself, others, God and the universe?
When did I have the least sense of belonging?

When was I happiest today?
When was I saddest?

What was today's high point?
What was today's low point?
—DENNIS LINN, SHEILA FABRICANT LINN, MATTHEW LINN

LESSON

There is no place in the Art of Peace for pettiness and selfish thoughts. Rather than being captivated by the notion of "winning or losing," seek the true nature of things. Your thoughts should reflect the grandeur of the universe, a realm beyond life and death.[65]
—MORIHEI UESHIBA

AFFIRMATION & INTENTION

It is a species of jealousy. We dislike to believe that anybody else is quite as good as we are . . . As for me, I choose to stop following this current, to stop posing as the judge of the universe.

If it brought any good results I might continue, but to date it has carried me out into the desert and left me there.

I choose another road for myself. I choose to look at people through God, using God as my glasses, colored with divine love for them.[66]

—Frank C. Laubach

PRAYER

The Metta Sutta

This is what should be done
by one who is skilled in goodness,
and who knows the path of peace:
Wishing:
in gladness and in safety,
may all beings be at ease.
May they be joyous and live in safety!
All beings, whether weak or strong—omitting none—
in high, middle, or low realms of existence,
small or great, visible or invisible,
near or far away, born or to be born—
may all beings be happy and at their ease!
Let none deceive another,
or despise any being in any state!

Let none by anger or ill-will wish harm to another!
Even as a mother watches over and protects her child, her only child,
so with a boundless heart
should one cherish all living beings:
radiating kindness over the entire world,
spreading upwards to the skies,
and downwards to the depths;
outwards and unbounded,
freed from hatred and ill-will.[67]
—The Buddha, 6th or 5th century BCE

ADDITIONAL READINGS ABOUT FORGIVING OTHERS

Forgiveness is simply release into the Spirit. . . .

Forgiveness is not forgetting or allowing hurt to continue. That's because forgiveness is not the same thing as reconciliation. Reconciliation is restoration of relationship. With forgiveness, the Spirit might lead us to reconcile—but might not as well. . . .

Forgiveness as release is not about getting anything from someone else. It is not dependent on others' actions or feelings. Forgiveness as release happens between an individual and the source of all Mercy. Walking this path, we avoid conditional thinking: "I'll forgive when they express remorse, face just consequences, hurt like I do . . . " or any other way we wish others would "pay" for their wrongs. Forgiveness as release aims to be more holistic than legalistic or performative. . . .

Forgiveness means that I am no longer bound by what happened to me; the offense no longer exerts power over me. . . .

Sometimes I test my willingness: Am I willing to be willing to forgive? Usually. Am I willing to forgive? Okay, maybe if . . . And I might simmer there for a while. Nothing wrong with that. I notice what I'm feeling. I can sit compassionately with reality and the Spirit. I can ask: What am I believing about the situation, myself, my feelings? Is that true? Really? I remember not to believe everything I think![68]

—CHRISTINE BETZ HALL

Not forgiving is like drinking rat poison and then waiting for the rat to die.[69]

—ANNE LAMOTT

My religion is kindness.[70]

—DALAI LAMA

The responsibility of tolerance lies with those who have the wider vision.[71]
—George Eliot, 1860

Every judgment of the other person is importantly a self-judgment.[72]
—Howard Thurman

"Doesn't your story have some kind of a moral or a point to it?"
"There's no explaining human behavior, honey. You just look at it."[73]
—Linda Raymond

Let us then try what love can do.[74]
—William Penn, 1693

Healing, health, and aging

SETTLING THE DAY

Ask yourself:

When did I give and receive the most love today?
When did I give and receive the least love today?

When did I feel most alive today?
When did I most feel life draining out of me?

When today did I have the greatest sense of belonging to myself, others, God and the universe?
When did I have the least sense of belonging?

When was I happiest today?
When was I saddest?

What was today's high point?
What was today's low point?
—Dennis Linn, Sheila Fabricant Linn, Matthew Linn

LESSON

Daily chant in Buddhist monastery:

Breathing in and out, I am aware of the fact that I am of the nature to die; I cannot escape dying.
I am of the nature to grow old; I cannot escape old age.
I am of the nature to get sick. Because I have a body, I cannot avoid sickness.
Everything I cherish, treasure and cling to today, I will have to abandon one day.[75]

—THÍCH NHẤT HẠNH

Hạnh comments: We must recognize this reality and smile.

AFFIRMATION & INTENTION

The Divine Milieu is a very personal and autobiographical book in which the author speaks of what he calls, in the first half of life, "divinizing one's activities," and of "divinizing one's passivities" or "hallowing one's diminishments" in the second half. These are numinous words, "divinizing" and "hallowing." To divinize one's activities would be to grow in consciousness that one's gifts are just that, they have been given one by the giver of all good things, God . . .

Consulting the dictionary, I find that for the word "hallowing" the following definitions are offered: "make holy or set apart for holy use, consecrate; to respect greatly; venerate." It was a new and most encouraging idea to me—that one's diminishments could be "made holy," "consecrated," "respected greatly," even "venerated."

I saw that the first step for me in learning to "hallow" the progressive diminishments in store for me was a deep-going acceptance.[76]

—JOHN YUNGBLUT

PRAYER

Whether I live or die, I belong to God.[77]

—ROMANS

SETTLING THE DAY

Ask yourself:

When did I give and receive the most love today?
When did I give and receive the least love today?

When did I feel most alive today?
When did I most feel life draining out of me?

When today did I have the greatest sense of belonging to myself, others, God and the universe?
When did I have the least sense of belonging?

When was I happiest today?
When was I saddest?

What was today's high point?
What was today's low point?
—Dennis Linn, Sheila Fabricant Linn, Matthew Linn

LESSON

All gifts of nature and of grace have been given us on loan. The ownership is not ours, but God's. God never gave personal property to anyone . . . in any way. Treat all things as if they are loaned to you . . . whether body or soul, sense or strength, external goods or honors, friends or relations, house or hall, everything.[78]
—Meister Eckhart, c. 1260–1328

AFFIRMATION & INTENTION

Each fifteen or twenty-minute attempt to go into the silence [worship]. . . involves a conscious exercise in "letting go." . . . an intentional letting go of one's waning gifts and talents, a committing of them into the care of the giver of all good things and a rededication of what creative potential remains.[79]

—JOHN YUNGBLUT

PRAYER

Be merciful to me, God, for I am in distress; my eyes grow weak with sorrow, my soul and body with grief . . . I am forgotten as a dead man out of mind; I am like something given up for lost . . . But I trust in you; I say, "You are my God." My times are in your hands.[80]

—THE PSALMS

SETTLING THE DAY

Ask yourself:

When did I give and receive the most love today?
When did I give and receive the least love today?

When did I feel most alive today?
When did I most feel life draining out of me?

When today did I have the greatest sense of belonging to myself, others, God and the universe?
When did I have the least sense of belonging?

When was I happiest today?
When was I saddest?

What was today's high point?
What was today's low point?
—Dennis Linn, Sheila Fabricant Linn, Matthew Linn

LESSON

We have to accept that things like this do happen and will happen. Suffering is built into life; it's part of life, as death is part of life. They are part of the whole scheme of things that makes life possible, even if we cannot understand how or why . . .

Our care and the process of healing or restoration gives meaning to the pain. The pain and suffering do not entirely disappear, but they are supported and held by the love that can embrace them and the good they make possible . . .

When you accept your faults and failings with total openness and honesty in the presence of God, you find you are accepted. That is grace. Similarly, when you accept your sufferings as part of life, part of the gift of life, you find you are accepted. You are held and embraced. The pain is still there, but you don't feel it in the same way. In fact you feel life in a new way. When you embrace suffering and death as part of life, you are accepting life itself, which is the other side of death. And life responds. You come to life, even amid the tears and the heartache.[81]

—Rex Ambler

AFFIRMATION & INTENTION

Many are my defeats, yet how many my deliverances! After servitude to [say what has ensnared you] I choose service to God; after exile in Babylon, I rebuild God's shrine; yesterday's wounds—so nearly fatal—begin to heal and I, living still, plant new seeds for renewal of my connection to God and a godly life.[82]

—Jewish prayer

PRAYER

Prayer for Healing

Thy name is my healing, O my God, and remembrance of Thee is my remedy. Nearness to Thee is my hope, and love for Thee is my companion. Thy mercy to me is my healing and my succor in both this world and the world to come. Thou, verily, art the All-Bountiful, the All-Knowing, the All-Wise.[83]

—Bahá'u'lláh, c. 1873

SETTLING THE DAY

Ask yourself:

When did I give and receive the most love today?
When did I give and receive the least love today?

When did I feel most alive today?
When did I most feel life draining out of me?

When today did I have the greatest sense of belonging to myself, others, God and the universe?
When did I have the least sense of belonging?

When was I happiest today?
When was I saddest?

What was today's high point?
What was today's low point?
—Dennis Linn, Sheila Fabricant Linn, Matthew Linn

LESSON

"You know what they say," he continued. "At our age, if you awake with no pain you're probably dead."

Again laughter.[84]

—Yewande Omotoso

AFFIRMATION & INTENTION

This, too, shall pass.[85]
—Suft Farid al-Din Attar, 13th century

PRAYER

Prayer Before Surgery

Strengthen me, O God, to do what I have to do and bear what I have to bear; that, accepting your healing gifts through the skill of surgeons and nurses, I may be restored to usefulness in your world with a thankful heart; and this I pray.

Amen.[86]

—AUTHOR UNKNOWN

ADDITIONAL READINGS ABOUT HEALTH, HEALING, AND AGING

"What's so funny?"

"I was just thinking about how much easier life is when you're young."

Ethan gave him a look of severe reproach. "There's nothing easy about being young, Doctor. If you think there is, then you've got a lousy memory."

"No, I don't, son. Now, you don't have to tell me if this fits you, but when I was young, I knew all the answers. Or, at least, I knew the answers were lying around, waiting to be found if I looked hard enough for 'em. Then, the older I got, the fewer answers and the more questions I had. Eventually, you've got all questions and no answers. And that's what's easy about being young."[87]

—Howard Weinstein

The Lord heals the broken of heart, and binds up their wounds.[88]
—The Psalms

Oh God . . . , spirit of the universe, I am old in years and in the sight of others, but I do not feel old within myself . . .

Help me to loosen, fiber by fiber, the instinctive strings that bind me to the life I know. Infuse me with a spirit so that it is to Thee that I turn, not the old ropes of habit and thought. Make me poised and free . . . to go forward eagerly and joyfully into the new phase of life that we call death . . .

Give me joy in awaiting the great change that comes after this life of many changes; let my self be merged in Thy self as a candle's wavering light is caught up in the sun.[89]

—Elizabeth Gray Vining

Grief and mourning

SETTLING THE DAY

Review your day. Was there any time that you felt stuck or couldn't be the person you'd like to be?

When you see what the problem is, at that point bring it into the light . . . Sit still until you can feel the presence [of God], quiet and peaceful, and then introduce into that circle of light the difficult or ugly thing you wish to confront. In your persistent waiting for this moment of stillness and confidence, you will find and feel . . . the little "death" or pruning through which we relinquish something which blocks the formation of Christ* within.[90]
—Brian Drayton

If this change happens for you tonight, give thanks.

If it does not, don't worry. Take a moment to notice what happened today for which you can be thankful.

*The word "Christ" used in this way by some modern Friends (Quakers) does not necessarily refer to Jesus of Nazareth. Instead, for many Quaker writers including the author of this reading, it means the light of God, the source of creation. This includes the divine light in each of us, which Friends see as our inner teacher and guide, no matter our spiritual path or religion or lack of one.

LESSON

Nature often offers metaphors more elegant than any we can manufacture. In the redwood ecosystem, all seeds are contained in pods called burls, tough brown clumps that grow where the mother tree's trunk and root system meet. When the mother tree is logged, blown over, or destroyed by fire the trauma stimulates the burls' growth hormones. The seeds release, and trees sprout around her, creating the circle of daughters. The daughter trees grow by absorbing the sunlight their mother cedes to them when she dies. And they get the moisture and nutrients they need from their mother's root system, which remains intact even after her leaves die. Although the daughters exist independently of their mother above ground, they continue to draw sustenance from her underneath.

I am fooling only myself when I say my mother exists now only in the photograph on my bulletin board or in the outline of my hand or in the armful of memories I still hold tight. She lives on beneath everything I do. Her presence influenced who I was, and her absence influences who I am. Our lives are shaped as much by those who leave us as they are by those who stay. Loss is our legacy. Insight is our gift. Memory is our guide.[91]

—Hope Edelman

AFFIRMATION & INTENTION

In what watered, ever-blissful gardens, on what trees, from what flower-goblets, gently stripped of petals, do these exotic fruits of consolation ripen? These luscious fruits—you might find one in the trampled meadow of your loss. And time and time again you wonder: at the size of the fruit, its firm well-being, the smoothness of its skin.[92]

—Rainer Maria Rilke

PRAYER

God, You give us dear ones and make them the strength of our life, the light of our eyes. They depart from us and leave us bereaved; but You are the living source of our healing. To You the stricken look for comfort and the sorrow-laden for consolation. . . . we see life as through windows that open on eternity. We see that love abides, the soul abides, as You, O God, abide, forever. We see that our years are more than grass that withers, more than flowers that fade. They weave a pattern of life that is limitless and unite us with a world that is from end to end the abode of Your love . . . In life and in death we cannot go where You are not, and where You are, all is well.[93]

—Jewish prayer

SETTLING THE DAY

Review your day. Was there any time that you felt stuck or couldn't be the person you'd like to be?

When you see what the problem is, at that point bring it into the light . . . Sit still until you can feel the presence [of God], quiet and peaceful, and then introduce into that circle of light the difficult or ugly thing you wish to confront. In your persistent waiting for this moment of stillness and confidence, you will find and feel . . . the little "death" or pruning through which we relinquish something which blocks the formation of Christ* within.
—BRIAN DRAYTON

If this change happens for you tonight, give thanks.

If it does not, don't worry. Take a moment to notice what happened today for which you can be thankful.

*The word "Christ" used in this way by some modern Friends (Quakers) does not necessarily refer to Jesus of Nazareth. Instead, for many Quaker writers including the author of this reading, it means the light of God, the source of creation. This includes the divine light in each of us, which Friends see as our inner teacher and guide, no matter our spiritual path or religion or lack of one.

LESSON

Life is a trust, given into our hands, to hold carefully, to use well, to enjoy, to give back when the time comes.[94]
—ELIZABETH GRAY VINING

AFFIRMATION & INTENTION

Dying can bring one of love's finest moments. We let our loved one go. We help them feel free to go.[95]
—SHULAMITH CLEARBRIDGE

PRAYER

Only For a Short While

Oh, only for so short a while you
have loaned us to each other,
because we take form in your act of drawing us,
and we take life in your painting us,
and we breathe in your singing us.

But only for so short a while
have you loaned us to each other.
Because even a drawing cut in obsidian fades,
and the green feathers, the crown feathers,
of the Quetzal bird lose their color,
and even the sounds of the waterfall
die out in the dry season.

So, we too, because only for a short while
have you loaned us to each other.[96]
—Aztec prayer

SETTLING THE DAY

Review your day. Was there any time that you felt stuck or couldn't be the person you'd like to be?

When you see what the problem is, at that point bring it into the light . . . Sit still until you can feel the presence [of God], quiet and peaceful, and then introduce into that circle of light the difficult or ugly thing you wish to confront. In your persistent waiting for this moment of stillness and confidence, you will find and feel . . . the little "death" or pruning through which we relinquish something which blocks the formation of Christ* within.
—BRIAN DRAYTON

If this change happens for you tonight, give thanks.

If it does not, don't worry. Take a moment to notice what happened today for which you can be thankful.

*The word "Christ" used in this way by some modern Friends (Quakers) does not necessarily refer to Jesus of Nazareth. Instead, for many Quaker writers including the author of this reading, it means the light of God, the source of creation. This includes the divine light in each of us, which Friends see as our inner teacher and guide, no matter our spiritual path or religion or lack of one.

LESSON

Sometimes religion appears to be presented as offering easy cures for pain: have faith and God will mend your hurts; reach out to God and your woundedness will be healed. The Beatitude "Blessed are they who mourn, for they shall be comforted" can be interpreted this way too, but the Latin root of the word "comfort" means "with strength" rather than "at ease." The Beatitude is not promising to take away our pain; indeed the inference is that the pain will remain with us. It does promise that God will cherish us and our wound, and help us draw a blessing from our distressed state.[97]
—S. JOCELYN BURNELL

AFFIRMATION & INTENTION

Gradually I learned one more thing, quite simple and obvious to many but hidden from me at first; that grief is something not to overcome or to escape but to live with. It is always there, as perceptible as a person who will not go away in spite of hints or plain speaking, but one can make room for it, recognize it as a companion instead of an intruder, be aware of it but not possessed by it; one can continue one's work, one's occupation, even one's joys, in its presence.[98]
—Elizabeth Gray Vining

PRAYER

God redeems my soul in peace from the battle waged against me. Gladness and joy will overtake me.

You will turn my sorrow into dancing. You will remove my sackcloth and clothe me with joy. You will turn the curse into a blessing.

Peace, peace to those far and near, says the Lord, and I will heal them. I will give strength to my people; I will bless my people with peace, and revive their hearts.

God will make my wilderness like Eden, and my desert a garden. Joy and gladness will be found there, thanksgiving and the sound of singing.[99]

—Jewish prayer

ADDITIONAL READINGS ABOUT GRIEF AND MOURNING

When we allow ourselves to mourn, we make way for a virtual onslaught of emotions: fear, resentment, abandonment, guilt. And anger.[100]

—Hope Edelman

Whether it be sorrow for our own loss or sorrow for the world's pain, we must learn how to shoulder the burden of it, to carry it . . . Somehow we must learn not only to meet it with courage, which is comparatively easy, but to bear it with serenity, which is more difficult, being not a single act but a way of living.[101]

—Elizabeth Gray Vining

Death alters the reality of our lives; the death of an intimate changes it completely. . . . Life consisted of one rending novelty after another, as anyone who has lost a spouse can attest.

Still, as time went on, some of those novelties proved to be blessings. . . . So while on one hand there is my darling Drew, whom I will never cease to love and never cease to long for, on the other hand, there is a wonderful life that I enjoy and am grateful for.

I can't make those two realities—what I've lost and what I've found—fit together in some type of pattern of divine causality. I just have to hold them on the one hand and on the other, just like that.[102]

—Kate Braestrup

Trials, frustration, and patience

SETTLING THE DAY

Review your day. Was there any time that you felt stuck or couldn't be the person you'd like to be?

When you see what the problem is, at that point bring it into the light . . . Sit still until you can feel the presence [of God], quiet and peaceful, and then introduce into that circle of light the difficult or ugly thing you wish to confront. In your persistent waiting for this moment of stillness and confidence, you will find and feel . . . the little "death" or pruning through which we relinquish something which blocks the formation of Christ* within.
—Brian Drayton

If this change happens for you tonight, give thanks.

If it does not, don't worry. Take a moment to notice what happened today for which you can be thankful.

*The word "Christ" used in this way by some modern Friends (Quakers) does not necessarily refer to Jesus of Nazareth. Instead, for many Quaker writers including the author of this reading, it means the light of God, the source of creation. This includes the divine light in each of us, which Friends see as our inner teacher and guide, no matter our spiritual path or religion or lack of one.

LESSON

Adaptation:

And Friends, though you may have tasted of God's power, and been convinced of the truth of it, and have felt the light, yet afterwards you may feel winter storms, tempests, and hail, and be frozen, in frost and cold and a wilderness and temptations.

Be patient and still in the power, and be still in the light, and they will convince you again. Keep your minds quietly on God, that you may come to the summer; don't flee from God because it is winter in your spirit.

For if you sit still in the patience which overcomes difficulties by the power of God, there will be no fleeing. For the farmer sows seed and then is patient. For by the power and by the light you will come to see through, and feel victorious over, winter storms and tempests, and all the coldness, barrenness, and emptiness.

And so if you hold steady in the light, you will know God's strength, you will feel the gentle rain, you will feel the fresh springs of life in the power and light, if you stay humble.

In the power and light God will reveal secrets, inspiring you and bringing you gifts through which your hearts will be filled with divine love. And so feel the promise and blessing of God set over all.

—George Fox, 1656

Original:

And Friends, though you may have tasted of the power and been convinced and have felt the light, yet afterwards you may feel winter storms, tempests, and hail, and be frozen, in frost and cold and a wilderness and temptations.

Be patient and still in the power and still in the light that doth convince you, to keep your minds to God; in that be quiet, that you may come to the summer, that your flight be not in the winter.

For if you sit still in the patience which overcomes in the power of God, there will be no flying. For the husbandman, after he hath sown his seed, he is patient. For by the power and by the light you will come to see through and feel over winter storms, tempests, and all the coldness, barrenness, emptiness . . .

And so in the light standing still you will see your salvation, you will see the Lord's strength, you will feel the small rain, you will feel the fresh springs in the power and light, your minds being kept low . . .

But in the power and light you will see God revealing His secrets, inspiring, and His gifts coming to you, through which your hearts will be filled with God's love . . . And so feel that over all set, which hath the promise and blessing of God.[103]

AFFIRMATION & INTENTION

Give thanks for unknown blessings already on their way.[104]
—Native American proverb

PRAYER

Prayer Before Sleep

Thank You for today. Thank You for . . .

[*Think about your day and give thanks for each good thing that happened.*]

[*If you are troubled or ill, add:*]
I wish/need/pray that during the night . . .
[*Specify your needs*]

and I will awaken . . .
[*Specify your needs.*]

Thank You.
Thank You.[105]
—Shulamith Clearbridge

SETTLING THE DAY

Review your day. Was there any time that you felt stuck or couldn't be the person you'd like to be?

When you see what the problem is, at that point bring it into the light . . . Sit still until you can feel the presence [of God], quiet and peaceful, and then introduce into that circle of light the difficult or ugly thing you wish to confront. In your persistent waiting for this moment of stillness and confidence, you will find and feel . . . the little "death" or pruning through which we relinquish something which blocks the formation of Christ* within.
—Brian Drayton

If this change happens for you tonight, give thanks.

If it does not, don't worry. Take a moment to notice what happened today for which you can be thankful.

*The word "Christ" used in this way by some modern Friends (Quakers) does not necessarily refer to Jesus of Nazareth. Instead, for many Quaker writers including the author of this reading, it means the light of God, the source of creation. This includes the divine light in each of us, which Friends see as our inner teacher and guide, no matter our spiritual path or religion or lack of one.

LESSON

Adaptation:

Blessed are they who going through the valley of misery use it for a well. God has promised, not that we shall be free from difficulties and challenges, rather do they form the ladder by which the soul mounts upwards.

—Père Grou, 1731–1803

Original:

Blessed is the man . . . who going through the vale of misery use it for a well. . . . God has promised, not that he shall be free from crosses, rather do they form the ladder by which the soul mounts upwards.[106]

AFFIRMATION & INTENTION

These trees which we plant, and under whose shade we shall never sit, we love them for themselves, and for the sake of our children and our children's children, who are to sit beneath the shadow of their spreading boughs.[107]
—Hyacinthe Loyson, 1866

PRAYER

God of all mercies, please help me to see this trial as containing the blessings of experience, of increasing my strength and patience, and of bringing me closer to you in my need. Thank you.
—Shulamith Clearbridge

SETTLING THE DAY

Review your day. Was there any time that you felt stuck or couldn't be the person you'd like to be?

When you see what the problem is, at that point bring it into the light . . . Sit still until you can feel the presence [of God], quiet and peaceful, and then introduce into that circle of light the difficult or ugly thing you wish to confront. In your persistent waiting for this moment of stillness and confidence, you will find and feel . . . the little "death" or pruning through which we relinquish something which blocks the formation of Christ* within.
—BRIAN DRAYTON

If this change happens for you tonight, give thanks.

If it does not, don't worry. Take a moment to notice what happened today for which you can be thankful.

*The word "Christ" used in this way by some modern Friends (Quakers) does not necessarily refer to Jesus of Nazareth. Instead, for many Quaker writers including the author of this reading, it means the light of God, the source of creation. This includes the divine light in each of us, which Friends see as our inner teacher and guide, no matter our spiritual path or religion or lack of one.

LESSON

Let nothing disturb you,
Let nothing frighten you,
All things pass away:
God never changes.

Patience obtains all things.
One who has God
Finds they lack nothing;
God alone suffices.[108]
—TERESA OF AVILA, 1515–1582

AFFIRMATION & INTENTION

We shall steer safely through every storm, so long as our heart is right, our intention fervent, our courage steadfast, and our trust fixed on God. If at times we are somewhat stunned by the tempest, never fear. Let us take breath, and go on afresh.[109]

—Francis de Sales, 1567–1622

PRAYER

O Lord! Thou art on the sandbanks as well as in the midst of the current; I bow to thee.

Thou art in the little pebbles as well as the calm expanse of the sea; I bow to Thee.

O all-pervading Lord, Thou art in the barren soil and in the crowded places; I bow to Thee.[110]

—Hindu Veda

SETTLING THE DAY

Review your day. Was there any time that you felt stuck or couldn't be the person you'd like to be?

When you see what the problem is, at that point bring it into the light . . . Sit still until you can feel the presence [of God], quiet and peaceful, and then introduce into that circle of light the difficult or ugly thing you wish to confront. In your persistent waiting for this moment of stillness and confidence, you will find and feel . . . the little "death" or pruning through which we relinquish something which blocks the formation of Christ* within.
—Brian Drayton

If this change happens for you tonight, give thanks.

If it does not, don't worry. Take a moment to notice what happened today for which you can be thankful.

*The word "Christ" used in this way by some modern Friends (Quakers) does not necessarily refer to Jesus of Nazareth. Instead, for many Quaker writers including the author of this reading, it means the light of God, the source of creation. This includes the divine light in each of us, which Friends see as our inner teacher and guide, no matter our spiritual path or religion or lack of one.

LESSON

Marjorie Reed changed my life when she said to me, "We live in the most friendly universe!" I decided that was the kind of universe I wanted and, with a lot of work, eventually transformed my expectations. And I got that universe.[111]
—Shulamith Clearbridge

AFFIRMATION & INTENTION

I wish to see that the universe is friendly to me. My experience tells me otherwise, but I am determined to free my future from the past by learning to expect the best. My past has shaped me and may always affect me in some ways. But I can decide to look forward with optimism. I can ask God to prove that our universe is friendly. I can notice when it is. I can put little reminders here and there so I remember to look at life in this new way.
—Shulamith Clearbridge

PRAYER

God, give us grace to accept with serenity
the things that cannot be changed,
courage to change the things that should be changed,
and the wisdom to distinguish the one from the other.[112]
—Reinhold Niebuhr

This second stanza accompanies many adaptations of Niebuhr's prayer:

Grant me patience with the changes that take time,
appreciation of all that I have,
tolerance of those with different struggles,
and strength to get up and try again,
one day at a time.[113]
—Author unknown

ADDITIONAL READINGS ABOUT TRIALS, FRUSTRATION, AND PATIENCE

There are many moments when I can tell Adam [who has Down syndrome] is terribly frustrated by not being able to speak clearly. . . . There are many times when I see the pain on his face as he struggles to communicate. . . . But just at the moment when Adam's frustration is most intense and I expect to see him fall into rage or despair, something changes—or rather, Adam changes something. I don't know how to describe this, except that he appears to make a conscious choice to see the situation as ridiculous. He'll take a deep breath, as though he is letting the frustration slide off his shoulders, and begin to laugh.

This is not the laughter of an idiot. It is the laughter of a person who chooses to see humor in his own discouragement, and to me it is not only intelligent but wise. . . . He laughs at his own bizarre pronunciation, at the inaccurate attempts others make to understand him, at his strenuous efforts to communicate . . . He . . . [finds] his own plight—the plight that for me, the Harvard graduate, would be simply awful—awfully funny. . . .

His laugh is so belly-deep, so apropos, so genuine, that every person within earshot ends up laughing along with him.[114]

—Martha Beck

I beseech you not to grasp the knife of these current troubles and misfortunes by its sharp edge, lest you let it injure you that way, but rather, seizing it by its blunt side, use it to excise all the imperfections you may recognize in yourself; so that you rise above the obstacles . . . and in this fashion arrive at an awareness of the vanity and fallacy of all earthly things: seeing and touching with your own hands the truth that neither the love of your children, nor pleasures, honors or riches can confer true contentment, being in themselves ephemeral; but only in blessed God . . . can we find real peace.[115]

—Maria Celeste Galilei, 1600–1630

If one is not in a hurry, even an egg will start walking.[116]
—Ethiopian proverb

When the sea comes calling . . . you give your house for a coral castle, and you learn to breathe underwater.[117]
—Sr. Carol Bialock, RSCJ

At our Meeting in India at the Quaker International Center in Delhi there were rarely more than five or six Quakers present. The rest were Hindus, Sikhs, Christians of various sects, Seekers [*sic*] attached to no particular religion, and occasionally a Muslim or Buddhist. During the difficult months when he was attempting to prevent a break between Hindu and Muslim in independent India, Gandhi used to attend this Meeting . . . its strength really lay in the readiness of [people] of all faiths to gather together in silence, confident that the light would break in upon them and that some of it would emerge in words that would enlarge and strengthen the spirits of all.

Often a Christian, a Hindu and a Sikh would speak to the same opening of truth in a way which would enlarge horizons for everyone.[118]

—Bradford Smith

Let your mind be quiet, realising the beauty of the world,
and the immense, the boundless treasures that it holds in store.
All that you have within you, all that your heart desires,
all that your nature so specially fits you for—
that or the counterpart of it waits embedded
in the great Whole, for you.
It will surely come to you.
Yet equally surely not one moment
before its appointed time will it come.

All your crying and fever and reaching out of hands
will make no difference.
Therefore do not begin that game at all.
Do not recklessly spill the waters of your mind
in this direction and in that,
lest you become like a spring lost and dissipated in the desert.

But draw them together into a little compass,
and hold them still, so still;
and let them become clear, so clear—so limpid, so mirror-like;
at last the mountains and the sky shall glass themselves
in peaceful beauty,
and the antelope shall descend to drink and to gaze
at her reflected image,
and the lion to quench his thirst,
and Love itself shall come and bend over and catch
its own lightness in you.[119]
—Edward Carpenter, 1883

Anger

SETTLING THE DAY

Review your day. Was there any time that you felt stuck or couldn't be the person you'd like to be?

When you see what the problem is, at that point bring it into the light . . . Sit still until you can feel the presence [of God], quiet and peaceful, and then introduce into that circle of light the difficult or ugly thing you wish to confront. In your persistent waiting for this moment of stillness and confidence, you will find and feel . . . the little "death" or pruning through which we relinquish something which blocks the formation of Christ* within.
—Brian Drayton

If this change happens for you tonight, give thanks.

If it does not, don't worry. Take a moment to notice what happened today for which you can be thankful.

*The word "Christ" used in this way by some modern Friends (Quakers) does not necessarily refer to Jesus of Nazareth. Instead, for many Quaker writers including the author of this reading, it means the light of God, the source of creation. This includes the divine light in each of us, which Friends see as our inner teacher and guide, no matter our spiritual path or religion or lack of one.

LESSON

I can reject an emotion. Not deny it, but ask myself, What will this incident mean in 300 years? Then the cause of it seems irrelevant, and the feeling dissipates. Or I can change it by imagining I'm rising up, flying above the world, until I'm high enough that my perspective changes and the problem then seems very small. Or the emotion will change if I can find gratitude about some part or aftereffect of it, finding a blessing in the situation.[120]
—Shulamith Clearbridge

AFFIRMATION & INTENTION

Adaptation:

It is reasonable and right for me to serve God diligently even when God does not help me. This continual service is as profitable to me as when God does help me, though I cannot see it.

And though this is very difficult for my hasty will, it is indeed the true worship.

—James Nayler, written while in prison, 1664

Original:

My waitings upon him when he moves not is my reasonable service, and a profiting time to me as if he moved, though I see it not, and this I found a great cross to my hasty will, which indeed is the true worship in Spirit.[121]

PRAYER

Peace is, above all things, a state of the will.[122]
—Evelyn Underhill

Help me to live, work, and endure in peace.

SETTLING THE DAY

Review your day. Was there any time that you felt stuck or couldn't be the person you'd like to be?

When you see what the problem is, at that point bring it into the light . . . Sit still until you can feel the presence [of God], quiet and peaceful, and then introduce into that circle of light the difficult or ugly thing you wish to confront. In your persistent waiting for this moment of stillness and confidence, you will find and feel . . . the little "death" or pruning through which we relinquish something which blocks the formation of Christ* within.
—Brian Drayton

If this change happens for you tonight, give thanks.

If it does not, don't worry. Take a moment to notice what happened today for which you can be thankful.

*The word "Christ" used in this way by some modern Friends (Quakers) does not necessarily refer to Jesus of Nazareth. Instead, for many Quaker writers including the author of this reading, it means the light of God, the source of creation. This includes the divine light in each of us, which Friends see as our inner teacher and guide, no matter our spiritual path or religion or lack of one.

LESSON

To injure an opponent is to injure yourself. To control aggression without inflicting injury is the Art of Peace.[123]
—Morihei Ueshiba

AFFIRMATION & INTENTION

May these hands be an instrument of peace.
May this mouth speak only pleasing words, healing words,
truthful words.
May I long for the sweet fragrance of sanctity,
May my face shine with the light of compassion.
May my eyes see the work of God everywhere I look,
May my ears hear only the resonance of the Creator,
May my neck bend in humility to the One,
May these feet walk on holy ground.[124]
—Sufi Ablution Prayers

I say the last line this way: May I recognize that I walk on holy ground.

PRAYER

Let my thoughts be gentle, my acts gracious; may kindness rule my lips and heart. Blessed is the spirit—a hymn of love within me, that calls me to prayer.[125]
—Jewish prayer

SETTLING THE DAY

Review your day. Was there any time that you felt stuck or couldn't be the person you'd like to be?

When you see what the problem is, at that point bring it into the light . . . Sit still until you can feel the presence [of God], quiet and peaceful, and then introduce into that circle of light the difficult or ugly thing you wish to confront. In your persistent waiting for this moment of stillness and confidence, you will find and feel . . . the little "death" or pruning through which we relinquish something which blocks the formation of Christ* within.
—Brian Drayton

If this change happens for you tonight, give thanks.

If it does not, don't worry. Take a moment to notice what happened today for which you can be thankful.

*The word "Christ" used in this way by some modern Friends (Quakers) does not necessarily refer to Jesus of Nazareth. Instead, for many Quaker writers including the author of this reading, it means the light of God, the source of creation. This includes the divine light in each of us, which Friends see as our inner teacher and guide, no matter our spiritual path or religion or lack of one.

LESSON

Be suspicious of yourself! Inquire about your hidden motives. It takes courage to repent, and more courage to change.[126]
—Jalaluddin Rumi

AFFIRMATION & INTENTION

Sophia: Anger is a lot like a piece of shredded wheat caught under your dentures. If you leave it there, you'll get a blister and have to eat jello all week. If you get rid of it, the sore heals, and you feel better.

Dorothy: Anger is like a piece of shredded wheat?

Sophia: If you want poetry, you listen to Neal Diamond. If you want good advice, you listen to your mother.[127]

—Episode of *Golden Girls*

I will not let this anger fester until it blisters my heart. I will let it out, in a safe way, and try to figure out what it's telling me about myself.

PRAYER

Drop thy still dews of quietness
Till all our strivings cease;
Take from our souls the strain and stress,
And let our ordered lives confess
The beauty of thy peace.

Breathe through the heats of our desire
Thy coolness and thy balm;
Let sense be dumb, let flesh retire;
Speak through the earthquake, wind, and fire,
O still small voice of calm![128]
—John Greenleaf Whittier, 1872

ADDITIONAL READINGS ABOUT ANGER

Adaptation:

When her selfish part found itself called on the carpet by God, Catherine would pray: Even though it hurts, Your will be done: remove these ill-gotten benefits and give me Love—full, pure and sincere.

—St. Catherine of Genoa, 1447–1510

Original:

When her selfish part saw itself called out by Love, Catherine would turn to God and say: "Even though it pain sense, content Thy will: despoil me of this spoil and clothe me with Love—full, pure and sincere."[129]

Breathing in, I calm my whole body. Breathing out, I calm my whole body.[130]

—Buddhist Sutra

Our life is love, and peace, and tenderness; and bearing with one another, and forgiving one another . . . praying for one another, and helping one another up with a tender hand.[131]

—Isaac Penington, 1667

Humility

SETTLING THE DAY

The final format for settling the day uses quotations followed by Quaker "queries" to explore your day and your life. Each quotation and set of questions will be repeated for two days.

You see, love is one. Love is the whole. Love is an endless sea that you fall into. And once you fall into it, you can't fall out. It's not something you do. It's something that is done to you, and all you can do is let go.[132]
—Richard Rohr

What is most important in my life?
Is that what I deeply want to be most important?
Have I put "first things first" today?

LESSON

Adaptation:

And do stay humble, that the divine tree may take root in you downward and upward, so you grow straight, rooted and grounded into the rock of the Lord. You will be unmovable, so that storms and tempests cannot beat you down, so that when troubles and trials and affliction come, you will receive what you need from the Lord and know a sure strength. You will live in a pure peace which nothing can take from you.

So, my dear heart, remain humble and in awe of the Lord, and cling tightly to the Lord, that life no longer will be a heavy burden, and you will be free from what oppresses you, and that in you which hungers may be fed, and your thirsty soul may be satisfied.

—MARGARET FELL, 1657

Original:

And do keep low at the bottom, that the tree which cannot bring forth evil fruit, may take root downward and upward, that so thy growth may be true, rooted and grounded into the rock, unmovable, that the storms and tempests cannot beat down, that when troubles and trials and affliction come, thou may know a sure habitation, and portion, and living strength in the Lord, and a pure peace which cannot be taken from thee, so, my dear heart, low in the fear of the Lord wait, and keep fast to the Lord, that the heavy burden may be undone, and the oppressed may have freedom, and the hungry may have bread, and the soul that thirsts may be satisfied.[133]

AFFIRMATION & INTENTION

A monkey on a tree hurled a coconut at the head of a Sufi. The man picked it up, drank the milk, ate the flesh, and made a bowl from the shell.[134]

—ANTHONY DE MELLO, SJ

This story can be interpreted in many ways. De Mello comments: "Thank you for your criticism of me."

Another person might say, "When life gives you lemons, make lemonade."

I like to tell myself, "Find the blessing in this situation." Sometimes it takes quite a while before a blessing is evident. Often more blessings show up later.

PRAYER

This is my prayer to thee, my lord—
strike, strike at the root of penury in my heart.
Give me the strength lightly to bear my joys and sorrows.
Give me the strength to make my love fruitful in service.
Give me the strength never to disown the poor
or bend my knees before insolent might.
Give me the strength to raise my mind high above daily trifles.
And give me the strength to surrender my strength
to thy will with love.[135]
—Rabindranath Tagore

SETTLING THE DAY

You see, love is one. Love is the whole. Love is an endless sea that you fall into. And once you fall into it, you can't fall out. It's not something you do. It's something that is done to you, and all you can do is let go.
—Richard Rohr

What is most important in my life?
Is that what I deeply want to be most important?
Have I put "first things first" today?

LESSON

May I remember Whose I am and for Whom I am empowered to be at work.[136]
—Thomas R. Kelly

AFFIRMATION & INTENTION

Adaptation:

Let go of your own will; let go of running your life; let go of your own desire to know or to be anything; and sink down to the divine seed which God sows in the heart, and let that grow in you, and be in you, and breathe in you, and act in you, and you shall find by sweet experience that God recognizes that, and loves it, and takes responsibility for this seed, and will lead it to the full flourishing which is its inheritance.

—Isaac Penington, 1661

Original:

Give over thine own willing, give over thy own running, give over thine own desiring to know or be anything and sink down to the seed which God sows in the heart, and let that grow in thee and be in thee and breathe in thee and act in thee; and thou shalt find by sweet experience that the Lord knows that and loves and owns that, and will lead it to the inheritance of Life, which is its portion.[137]

PRAYER

We praise thee with our thoughts, O God. We praise thee even as the sun praises thee in the morning: may we find joy in being thy servants . . .

God made the rivers to flow. They feel no weariness, they never stop flowing. They move swiftly like birds in the air. May the stream of my life flow into the river of righteousness . . .

Cut off the bonds of afflictions that bind me: I cannot even open my eyes without thy help . . .

We will sing thy praises, O God almighty. We will now and evermore sing thy praises, even as they were sung of old . . .

Many mornings remain to dawn on us: lead us through them all, O God.[138]

—HINDU VEDA

SETTLING THE DAY

Divine love imposes no rigorous or unreasonable commands, but graciously points out the spirit of [loving one another] and the way to happiness, in the attaining of which it is necessary that we go forth out of all that is selfish.[139]
—JOHN WOOLMAN, 1720–1772

How do my possessions, and the means by which they were manufactured and acquired, affect other people and the natural environment?

Did the choices I made today match my vision for my life?
Were they selfish or selfless?[140]

LESSON

When Jesus came to earth as a baby,
he depended entirely upon human love—
that of Mary, Joseph and the shepherds.
When Jesus preached and healed,
he depended entirely upon human love—
the alms given by those who heard him.
I too depend on human love.
The kindness of others sustains my soul.
The gifts of others sustain my body.
Every person depends on others' love.
Let no one be ashamed of their needs.
To depend on others is to imitate Christ.[141]
—ROBERT VAN DE WEYER

AFFIRMATION & INTENTION

I will ask for help when I need it. Also, I recognize that it is a blessing to be able to help someone. In my need, I will be grateful to make this blessing possible for others.
—Shulamith Clearbridge

PRAYER

I can easily be proud of my accomplishments or positions and forget that whatever I have been given is not mine, but is Yours to be used for the service of others. Lord, teach me true humility.[142]
—Mary van Balen Holt

SETTLING THE DAY

Divine love imposes no rigorous or unreasonable commands, but graciously points out the spirit of [loving one another] and the way to happiness, in the attaining of which it is necessary that we go forth out of all that is selfish.
—John Woolman, 1720–1772

How do my possessions, and the means by which they were manufactured and acquired, affect other people and the natural environment?

Did the choices I made today match my vision for my life?

Were they selfish or selfless?

LESSON

I suffer from a chronic affliction. It is one to which physicians are particularly susceptible. The condition is seriosity. Seriosity produces an irresistible compulsion always to take oneself seriously. It is accompanied by the expectation that others will do the same. It is a most disagreeable condition, not only for those who are affected, but for everyone around them.

I have attempted several treatments to rid myself of seriosity. I have giggled in important meetings. I have sung nursery rhymes in hospital corridors. I have even paraded down Main Street dressed in outlandish outfits. None of these measures has succeeded. This book is my last hope, and it falls upon you, dear reader, to effect the cure that has so long eluded me. I hope you will not fail.[143]

—Beach Conger, MD

AFFIRMATION & INTENTION

To make a safe home for small children, to comfort one person in sorrow, to do one's work as efficiently as possible, to listen with understanding, to be gentle with the old and courteous to the young—these are the humble tasks to which most men and

women are called. They build the home or the meeting or the community which is the first step towards the Beloved Community. The second is to be aware of greater tasks and to be ready to be used in solving them—ready, not anxious or envious, but content to wait, exercising a ministry of prayer to sustain the healers and the reconcilers already at work in their thousands.[144]
—Olive Tyson

PRAYER

In Zimbabwe, one response to a greeting is "I am suffering peacefully."[145]
—Zimbabwean saying

Divine Guide and Kind Helper,
When times of suffering come, instead of my ranting and raging, show me how to suffer peacefully.
Thank you.

ADDITIONAL READINGS ABOUT HUMILITY

It is said that once Saint Teresa of Avila was riding through the back roads of Spain during a torrential rainstorm. The horse drawing her cart lost her footing and went down, and the cart slid into a stream, drenching Teresa and dumping out everything that had been loaded on the cart. Teresa complained to Jesus at being treated in this manner in the midst of trying to serve Him. The voice of Jesus then came to her from the heavens: "This is how I treat my friends." Wiping the mud from her face, she replied, "No wonder you have so few!"[146]
—Teresa of Avila

Stuff happens. It happens to everybody, even saints.

Who needs help? Every caregiver . . . . Even the best-equipped person needs respite. . . .

However reserved in your nature, however much you believe in self sufficiency, it is good to make your situation known and to open yourself to help. Taking help is not an imposition; it is a gift to the helper. It is a sign not of weakness but of strength . . . .

Ask for what you need, not just for your own sake, but for the sake of the person you are caring for. . . .

Asking for help enlarges your capacity and your spirit. If you keep resisting help, it is part of your spiritual work to discover what holds you back . . . Are you afraid of abandoning the person or of being abandoned? Have you fallen into . . . a secret belief that if you are a superhero—if only you keep doing absolutely everything—your person cannot die?[147]

—Patricia M. Nesbitt and Kristin Camitta Zimet

Let me have too deep a sense of humor ever to be proud.
Let me know my absurdity before I act absurdly.
Let me realize that when I am humble I am most human,
most truthful,
and most worthy of your serious consideration.[148]
—Daniel A. Lord, SJ

We must not drift away from the humble works, because these are the works nobody will do. It is never too small . . . therefore even if you write a letter for a blind man or you just go and sit and listen, or you take the mail for him, or you visit somebody or bring a flower to somebody—small things—or wash clothes for somebody, or clean the house. Very humble work, that is where you and I must be. For there are many people who can do big things. But there are very few people who will do the small things.[149]
—Mother Teresa

"Dear me!" said Mr. Omer, "when a man is drawing on to a time of life, where the two ends of life meet; when he finds himself, however hearty he is, being wheeled about for the second time, in a speeches [species] of go-cart; he should be over-rejoiced to do a kindness if he can. He wants [lacks] plenty. And I don't speak of myself, particular," said Mr. Omer, "because, sir, the way I look at it is, that we are all drawing on to the bottom of the hill, whatever age we are, on account of time never standing still for a single moment. So let us always do a kindness, and be over-rejoiced. To be sure!"[150]
—Charles Dickens, 1849–1850

By knocking at the door [of an ill person who would not want to see him], going in, making a fool of himself and coming out again, he prayed for that soul. As he knocked, his heart was beating faster than usual, but not so much with the habitual dread of making a fool of himself as with amazement and wonder at God's use of fools.[151]
—Elizabeth Goudge

[I wish to be one of] Those whom neither business nor striving after gain can turn from the remembrance of God, and from constancy in prayer, and from charity . . .[152]
—The Holy Qur'an

It is not the failure of others to appreciate your abilities that should trouble you, but rather your failure to appreciate theirs.[153]
—Confucius

Experience is a wonderful thing. It lets you recognize the same mistake when you make it again . . . and again until one day you stop making that bloomer.[154]
—Patrick Taylor

No one is completely useless. You can always serve as a bad example.[155]
— Jim Beaver

ZERO CIRCLE

Be helpless and dumbfounded,
unable to say yes or no.
Then a stretcher will come from grace
to gather us up.

We are too dull-eyed to see the beauty.
If we say *Yes we can*, we will be lying.
If we say *No, we don't see it*,
that No will behead us
and shut tight our window onto spirit.

So let us be not sure of anything,
besides ourselves, and only that,
so miraculous beings come running to help.
Crazed, lying in a zero circle, mute,
we will be saying finally,
with tremendous eloquence, *Lead us.*
When we have totally surrendered to that beauty,
we will become a mighty kindness.[156]
—Jalaluddin Rumi

God is here: comfort in the presence

SETTLING THE DAY

Adaptation:

Such who enter deeply into these considerations [about money and wealth] and live under the weight of them will feel the necessity of following divine wisdom, thereby to be directed in the right use of things, even if the promptings are in opposition to the customs of the times. We will be helped to bear patiently the reproaches we get because we act differently from everyone else.

—John Woolman

Original:

Such who enter deep into these considerations and live under the weight of them will feel . . . the necessity of attending singly to divine wisdom . . . thereby to be directed in the right use of things, in opposition to the customs of the times, and supported to bear patiently the reproaches attending singularity.[157]

Do I feel an urge to do things or live in ways that are very different from, or even conflict with, the society and culture around me?

Are there compensations that balance the consequences of being different from most people?

How do I bring myself to obey the still, small voice when I have strong reservations or fears?

LESSON

Just as the hand, held before the eye, can hide the tallest mountain, so the routine of every day life can keep us from seeing the vast radiance and the secret wonders that fill the world.[158]

—Rabbi Nachman of Bratslav, 1772–1810

AFFIRMATION & INTENTION

Imagine being in that Stream of Divine Presence which has been present in creation from the beginning of time.

Imagine being irradiated by the transforming love of God on all the secret and hidden levels of your being, even down all the corridors of memory.[159]

—William Tabor

PRAYER

How could the love between Thee and me sever?

As the leaf of the lotus abides on the water: so thou art my God, and I am Thy servant.

As the night-bird Chakor gazes all night at the moon: so Thou art my God and I am Thy servant.

From the beginning until the ending of time, there is love between Thee and me; and how shall such love be extinguished?

Kabir says: As the river enters into the ocean, so my heart touches Thee.[160]

—Kabir

SETTLING THE DAY

Adaptation:

Such who enter deeply into these considerations [about money and wealth] and live under the weight of them will feel the necessity of following divine wisdom, thereby to be directed in the right use of things, even if the promptings are in opposition to the customs of the times. We will be helped to bear patiently the reproaches we get because we act differently from everyone else.

—John Woolman

Original:

Such who enter deep into these considerations and live under the weight of them will feel . . . the necessity of attending singly to divine wisdom . . . thereby to be directed in the right use of things, in opposition to the customs of the times, and supported to bear patiently the reproaches attending singularity.[161]

Do I feel an urge to do things or live in ways that are very different, or even conflict with, the society and culture around me?

Are there compensations that balance the consequences of being different from most people?

How do I bring myself to obey the still, small voice when I have strong reservations or fears?

LESSON

Consider that you are in God, surrounded and encompassed by God, swimming in God.[162]

—Mother Teresa

AFFIRMATION & INTENTION

Know I am God.

I spoke to you at your first thought.
Be still
Know I am God.

I spoke to you at your first love.
Be still
Know I am God.

I spoke to you at your first song.
Be still
Know I am God.

I speak to you through the grass of the meadows.
Be still
Know I am God.

I speak to you through the trees of the forests.
Be still
Know I am God.

. . . .

I speak to you through the peace of the evening.
Be still
Know I am God.

. . . .

I speak to you through the storm and the clouds.
Be still
Know I am God.

. . . .

I will speak to you when you are alone
Be still
Know I am God.

I will speak to you through the Wisdom of the Ancients.
Be still
Know I am God.

I will speak to you at the end of time.
Be still
Know I am God.

. . . .

I will speak to you throughout Eternity.
Be still
Know I am God.

I speak to you.
Be still
Know I am God.[163]
—The Essene Gospel of Peace

PRAYER

May all I say and all I think
be in harmony with thee,
God within me,
God beyond me,
maker of the trees.[164]
—Chinook prayer

SETTLING THE DAY

My mind being affected herewith [by the conflict among Quakers about paying taxes to be used to fight wars], I had fresh opportunity to see and consider the advantage of living in the real substance of religion, where practice harmonizes with principle.[165]
—John Woolman

Did I strive today for awareness of God's continuing presence in my life?

Did I try to respond to "that of God"—the Divine Presence—in everyone, including those with whom I disagreed or by whom I have been hurt?

How can I free myself of discrimination and of prejudice? How can I learn to see all people as spiritual equals?[166]

LESSON

When we understand, we are at the center of the circle, and there we sit while Yes and No chase each other around the circumference.[167]
—Chuang-tzu, 300–200 BCE

AFFIRMATION & INTENTION

Adaptation:

The seed of the Blessed Community is sown and grows up in a way that we do not understand, and the power of God appears and works in it in a way of which we are not aware. We look for the Blessed Community, the power, and the life of the spirit in the way of our usual observation, according to the thoughts and expectations of our hearts. But it never comes this way, but rather in its own eternal way. It springs in the hearts of many of us, but we overlook it and turn away from it daily, not knowing its true appearance, but expecting it to be some other way. Thus we are held in the bonds of death, and we are captives in a strange land, refusing God's daily offers of life. And until we learn to see differently, we can never clearly perceive the presence of God.

—Isaac Penington

Original:

The seed of the kingdom is sown man knows not how, even by a sound of the eternal Spirit, which he is not a fit judge of; and it grows up he knows not how; and the power appears and works in it, in a way that he is not aware of. He looks for the kingdom, the power, and the life, in a way of his observation, answerable to the thoughts and expectations of his heart. But thus it never comes; but in the way of its own eternal motion, it springs in the hearts of many, and they overlook the thing, and turn from it daily, not knowing its proper way of appearance, but expecting it some other way. And thus the enemy holds them in the bands of death, and they are captives in the strange land, refusing the Prince of life, in his daily offers of life. . . . And till this eye of observation be put out in them, they can never clearly see the appearance of the Saviour to them.[168]

PRAYER

Sweet hymns and songs will I recite
To sing to You by day and night,
O You who are my soul's delight.

How does my soul within me yearn
Beneath Your shadow to return,
Your secret mysteries to learn.

And e'en while yet your glory fires
My words, and hymns of praise inspires,
Your love it is my heart desires.

My meditation day and night,
May it be pleasant in Your sight,
For You are all my soul's delight.[169]
—Jewish prayer

SETTLING THE DAY

My mind being affected herewith [by the conflict between Quakers about paying taxes to be used to fight wars], I had fresh opportunity to see and consider the advantage of living in the real substance of religion, where practice harmonizes with principle.
—John Woolman

Did I strive today for awareness of God's continuing presence in my life?

Did I try to respond to "that of God"—the Divine Presence—in everyone, including those with whom I disagreed or by whom I have been hurt?

How can I free myself of discrimination and of prejudice? How can I learn to see all people as spiritual equals?

LESSON

Here is something we can share with all of the people in the world. They cannot all be brilliant or rich or beautiful. They cannot all even dream beautiful dreams like God gives some of us . . . Their hearts do not all burn with love. But everybody can learn to hold God by the hand and rest. And when God is ready to speak, the fresh thoughts of heaven will flow in like a crystal spring. Everybody rests at the end of the day, what a world gain if everybody could rest in the waiting arms of our loving God, and listen until God whispers.[170]
—Frank C. Laubach

AFFIRMATION & INTENTION

Adaptation:

I will love the Lord with all my heart and with all my strength. I will teach this diligently to my children. I will remember it when I sit in my house, when I walk along the way, when I lie down and when I rise up. And God shall be in the work of my hands, and I will see God in everyone and in all of creation. I will imbue my home with the love of God, so all who come in may be blessed.

—Deuteronomy

Original:

You shall love the Lord your God with all your heart, with all your soul, and with all your strength. And these words which I command you today shall be in your heart. And you shall teach them diligently to your children, and shall talk of them when you sit in your house, when you walk by the way, when you lie down, and when you rise up. You shall bind them as a sign upon your hand, and they shall be as frontlets between your eyes. You shall write them upon the doorposts of your house and upon your gates.[171]

PRAYER

God be with our family, from the youngest to the oldest, lighting up our relationships, sowing grace into our troubles.

God be with our family, weaving love into our work, our rest, and our play.

Amen.[172]

—Julie Palmer

ADDITIONAL READINGS ABOUT GOD IS HERE: COMFORT IN THE PRESENCE

The same stream of life that runs through my veins night and day
runs through the world and dances in rhythmic measures.

It is the same life that shoots in joy through the dust of the earth
in numberless blades of grass and breaks into
tumultuous waves of leaves and flowers.

It is the same life that is rocked in the ocean-cradle of birth
and of death, in ebb and in flow.

I feel my limbs are made glorious by the touch of this world
of life. And my pride is from the life-throb of ages
dancing in my blood this moment.[173]
—Rabindranath Tagore

The soul is . . . in God, and God in the soul, as the fish is in the sea, and the sea in the fish.[174]
—Catherine of Siena, 1347–1380

The soul is kissed by God
in its innermost regions
with interior yearning,
grace and blessing are bestowed.[175]
—Hildegaard von Bingen

Invocation of Peace: After the Gaelic

Deep peace I breathe into you,
O weariness, here:
O ache, here!
Deep peace, a soft white dove to you;
Deep peace, a quiet rain to you;
Deep peace, an ebbing wave to you!
Deep peace, red wind of the east from you;
Deep peace, grey wind of the west to you;
Deep peace, dark wind of the north from you;
Deep peace, blue wind of the south to you!
Deep peace, pure red of the flame to you;
Deep peace, pure white of the moon to you;
Deep peace, pure green of the grass to you;
Deep peace, pure brown of the earth to you;
Deep peace, pure grey of the dew to you;
Deep peace, pure blue of the sky to you!
Deep peace of the running wave to you,
Deep peace of the flowing air to you,
Deep peace of the quiet earth to you,
Deep peace of the sleeping stones to you!
Deep peace of the Yellow Shepherd to you,
Deep peace of the Wandering Shepherdess to you,
Deep peace of the Flock of Stars to you,
Deep peace from the Son of Peace to you,
Deep peace from the heart of Mary to you,
And from Briget [*sic*] of the Mantle
Deep peace, deep peace![176]
—FIONA MACLEOD

When you bow deeply to the universe, it bows back; when you call out the name of God, it vibrates inside you.[177]
—MORIHEI UESHIBA

I unlatched the shutters. The light was as intense as a love affair. I was blinded, delighted, not just because it was warm and wonderful, but because nature measures nothing. Nobody needs this much sunlight. Nobody needs droughts, volcanoes, monsoons, tornadoes either, but we get them, because our world is as extravagant as a world can be. We are the ones obsessed by measurement. The world just pours it out.[178]
—Jeanette Winterson

Bhogobaan ekane ache,
Mother Teresa whispered in Bengali
as she went from bed to bed:
"God is here."[179]
—Anita Mathias

Gratitude

SETTLING THE DAY

Our gracious Creator cares and provides for all creatures. God's tender mercies are over us all and over all the world. And so far as God's love influences our minds, so far we . . . feel a desire to take hold of every opportunity to lessen the distresses of the afflicted and increase the happiness of all creation. Here we have a prospect of one common interest from which our own is inseparable: to turn all the treasures we possess into the channel of universal love becomes the business of our lives.[180]
—John Woolman

Did I listen patiently today and seek the truth that other people's opinions may contain for me?[181]

Did I avoid hurtful criticism?[182]

In all my dealings with others today, did I remember that I might be mistaken?[183]

Did I notice not only the needs and gifts of the people around me, but also my own?[184]

Did I see "that of God"—the Divine Presence—in everyone?[185]

LESSON

. . . And hold fast, all together, to the rope of God, and do not draw apart from one another. And remember with gratitude the blessings which God has bestowed on you.[186]
—The Holy Qur'an

AFFIRMATION & INTENTION

Evening Meditation

[*Take three deep breaths*]

Oh loving, vast God of all!
You are infinite wisdom, infinite satisfaction,
infinite peace.
Please accept my thanks
and teach me how to be fully thankful.

[*Think of several things that happened today
for which you give thanks*]

Please listen to my heart
and teach me to ask for the right things in order to be useful to You.

[*State your desires for tomorrow*]

Infinite Spirit of Love
I wish to be more like You
I wish to be fully myself
I wish to live up to my possibilities!
Amen.[187]
—Shulamith Clearbridge

PRAYER

Oludumare, oh Divine One! I give thanks to You, the one who is as near as my heartbeat, and more anticipated than my next breath. Let Your wisdom become one with this vessel as I lift my voice in thanks for Your love.[188]

—Yoruban prayer

SETTLING THE DAY

Our gracious Creator cares and provides for all creatures. God's tender mercies are over us all and over all the world. And so far as God's love influences our minds, so far we . . . feel a desire to take hold of every opportunity to lessen the distresses of the afflicted and increase the happiness of all creation. Here we have a prospect of one common interest from which our own is inseparable: to turn all the treasures we possess into the channel of universal love becomes the business of our lives.
—John Woolman

Did I listen patiently today and seek the truth that other people's opinions may contain for me?

Did I avoid hurtful criticism?

In all my dealings with others today, did I remember that I might be mistaken?

Did I notice not only the needs and gifts of the people around me, but also my own?

Did I see "that of God"—the Divine Presence—in everyone?

LESSON

Let us rise up and be thankful, for if we didn't learn a lot today, at least we learned a little, and if we didn't learn a little, at least we didn't get sick, and if we got sick, at least we didn't die; so, let us all be thankful.[189]
—The Buddha

AFFIRMATION & INTENTION

God our Creator, our centre, our friend,
we thank you for our good life,
for those who are dear to us,
for our dead, and for all who have helped and influenced us.
We thank you for the measure of freedom we have,
and the extent to which we control our lives;
and most of all we thank you for the faith that is in us,
for our awareness of you and our hope in you.
Keep us, we pray you, thankful and hopeful
And useful until our lives shall end.
Amen.[190]
—The Anglican Church in Aotearoa,
New Zealand and Polynesia

PRAYER

Breathe slowly and evenly. As you do, think the words that follow. Let them be true.

Breathe in:	You nourish me in all the ways I need
Breathe out:	You cleanse me in all the ways I need
Breathe in:	You nourish, nourish, nourish
Breathe out:	You cleanse, cleanse, cleanse
Breathe in:	You nourish, nourish, nourish
Breathe out:	You cleanse, cleanse, cleanse
Breathe in:	I'm listening for Your guidance
Breathe out:	Thank you
Breathe in:	I'm listening for Your guidance
Breathe out:	Thank you
Breathe in:	I'm listening for Your guidance
Breathe out:	Thank you
Breathe in:	You help me to be a blessing to others
Breathe out:	I bless, bless, bless
Breathe in:	You help me to be a blessing to others
Breathe out:	I bless, bless, bless
Breathe in:	You help me to be a blessing to others
Breathe out:	I bless, bless, bless
Breathe in:	You enlarge my capacity for joy
Breathe out:	I bless, bless, bless
Breathe in:	Thank you
Breathe out:	I bless, bless, bless
Breathe in:	Thank you
Breathe out:	I bless, bless, bless.[191]

—SHULAMITH CLEARBRIDGE

III. Resources

Endnotes

1. Tubman, "Quote by Harriet Tubman," https://www.goodreads.com/quotes/22972-twant-me-twas-the-lord-i-always-told-him-i. Also quoted in Heidish, *Woman Called Moses*, n.p.

2. Psalm 4:8. A combination of versions from The Anglican Church in Aotearoa, *New Zealand Prayer Book,* 181 and Lamsa, *Holy Bible,* 590.

3. Tagore, *Gitanjali*, #LXXXI.

4. Fox, *Journal,* 277. Alludes to *The Holy Bible,* Isaiah 40:31 (KJV): "They that wait upon the Lord shall renew their strength; they shall mount up with wings as eagles; they shall run, and not be weary; and they shall walk, and not faint."

5. Richard of Chichester in Elderton, "The Prayer of St. Richard of Chichester," https://faithhub.net/the-prayer-of-saint-richard/. Richard, Bishop of Chichester, reportedly said these words as he was dying. Other versions begin: "Of you three things I pray:" or "Dear Lord, three things I pray;" some use "Thee" instead of "you." Some versions say: "May I see Thee more clearly. . ."

6. Christian Compline Prayer. Adapted by Shulamith Clearbridge from a prayerbook used at the Immaculate Heart of Mary Abbey, Benedictine Congregation of Solesmes, Westfield, VT. Online in a slightly different translation in St. David and St Patrick Catholic Church, "Latin Compline, Octave for Easter, Sundays of Eastertide," https://stdavidandstpatrick.files.wordpress.com/2020/04/latin-compline-eastertide.pdf, page 5.

7. Psalm 19:15. Chouraqui, *Les Saumes,* 128. Excerpt translated by Shulamith Clearbridge.

8. Sarah Reynolds, "Unison Prayer of Dedication" (Middlebury United Church of Christ communion prayer for the fifth Sunday after Epiphany, 2019)

9. Ellwood, quoted in Vining, *World in Tune,* 69.

10. Nouwen in Collins, "Voices: Henri Nouwen on Joy," https://revcollins.com/2021/04/21/voices-henri-nouwen-on-joy/. Quoted in Nouwen, *Here and Now*, n.p.

11. Adapted from Adler and Davis, *Mahzor Avodat,* n.p. Digitized by the Open Siddur Project and available online at https://opensiddur.org/?p=27332.

12. Yearly Meeting of Quakers in Britain, *Quaker Faith & Practice*, entry 1.02. Paraphrased from statements contained in epistles of the Yearly Meeting

of Pennsylvania and the Jerseys, 1694 and 1695. Online at https://www.pym.org/faith-and-practice/extracts-writings-friends/advices/.

13. Havel, "The Kind of Hope," 181.

14. Harjo, *Conflict Resolution*, 109.

15. Psalm 119, abridged and adapted from NASB by Shulamith Clearbridge.

16. Penington, "To Friends of both the Chalfonts," http://www.qhpress.org/texts/penington/letter25.html.

17. Kelly, *Testament of Devotion*, 45.

18. The Anglican Church in Aotearoa, *New Zealand Prayer Book*, 184, changed into the first person singular.

19. Boyle, *Tattoos on the Heart*, 86.

20. Nayler, "Milk for Babes and Meat for Strong Men: A Feast of Fat Things: Wine well refined on the Lees," in *Works of James Nayler*, 148–49. Online at http://www.qhpress.org/texts/nayler/milkmeat.html.

21. Nayler, "Milk for Babes," 162–63.

22. Fox, *Journal*, 574–75.

23. Unpublished vocal ministry given to Clearbridge, 2007.

24. van Balen Holt, *Dwelling Place Within*, 123.

25. Psalm 127:2. "Night Prayer," in The Anglican Church in Aotearoa, *New Zealand Prayer Book*, 167.

26. Various versions of this story exist. One example is at Adsit, "Taoist Farmer Story," https://newventureswest.com/real-lesson-taoist-farmer-story/.

27. White, "7 Daily Prayers," https://www.beliefnet.com/faiths/prayer/7-daily-prayers-women-transform-prayer-life.aspx, para. 4.

28. Guidance received by Clearbridge. Unpublished journal, 2007.

29. Psalm 27. Combination of versions from NLT (available at https://www.biblegateway.com/passage/?search=psalm%2027&version=NLT) and Lamsa, *Holy Bible*, 600.

30. Julian of Norwich. Quoted in March, "Quotations," https://interruptingthesilence.com/2012/05/08/quotations-from-st-julian-of-norwich/.

31. Underhill, *Letters*, 147–48. This was written in 1917.

32. Hạnh, *No Death No Fear*, 96.

33. Twain, "Courage," http://www.twainquotes.com/Courage.html. Credited to Twain, *Pudd'nhead Wilson's Calendar*, n.p.

34. Stevenson, "Like a clock during a thunderstorm," https://spiritualquotes.org/enlightenment/like-clock-thunderstorm/.

35. Fox in Yearly Meeting of Quakers in Britain, *Quaker Faith and Practice*, entry 20.23.

36. Bahauddin, *Drowned Book*, 79.

37. Smiley, *Good Faith*, 180.

38. Mother Teresa, "Quote by Mother Teresa," https://www.goodreads.com/quotes/663294-god-doesn-t-ask-that-we-succeed-in-everything-but-that. Included in Mother Teresa, *Joy in Loving*, n.p.

39. Private conversation with Shulamith Clearbridge.

40. "Great Spirit Prayer," translated by Lakota Chief Yellow Lark in 1887.

Available at Jesuit Resource, "Native American Prayers," https://www.xavier.edu/jesuitresource/online-resources/prayer-index/native-american.

41. Rubin, *Compassion and Self-Hate*, 231.

42. Van de Weyer, *Celtic Praise*, 55.

43. Shange, *for colored girls*, 63.

44. Loukes, cited in Steere, *Traveling In*, 29.

45. Underhill, *Letters*, 66–67, 96–97.

46. "A Liturgy for First Responders," in McKelvey, *Every Moment Holy*, 43.

47. Fox, "Epistle #16," https://qbi.earlham.edu/gfe/e001-020.htm#e16.

48. "Learning to Sit With Not Knowing," track 1 on Carrie Newcomer, *The Point of Arrival*, Carrie Newcomer Music (BMI), BMG Chrysalis, 2019.

49. "A Liturgy for The Hours: Midday," in McKelvey, *Every Moment Holy*, 8.

50. Wiser in Yearly Meeting of Quakers in Britain, *Quaker Faith and Practice*, entry 21.16.

51. Eckhart, *Meditations*, 127.

52. Ueshiba, *Art of Peace*, 133. Ueshiba was the founder of Aikido, the peaceful martial art and way of life.

53. Weinstein, *The Better Man*, 231.

54. Kabir, "V," in *One Hundred Poems*, 4. I have replaced the words "Brother" and "Sadhu" with "friend."

55. Chapman, quoted in Vining, *World in Tune*, 111.

56. Chapman, quoted in Vining, *World in Tune*, 121. Chapman also said: "The only way to pray is to pray, and the way to pray well is to pray much." (Sr. Dorsee, "The only way to pray is to pray . . . ," https://witnessestohope.org/2011/06/14/the-only-way-to-pray-is-to-pray/, para. 6.)

57. Nesbitt and Zimet, *A Tender Time*, 83–84.

58. May, *Awakened Heart*, 125.

59. Lamott, *Traveling Mercies*, 213.

60. Prejean, *Dead Man Walking*, 245.

61. Clearbridge, "Prayers for Healing After Trauma." In a slightly different form in Clearbridge, *Finding God*, 101.

62. Spickard Keeler, "Misunderstanding Forgiveness," https://quietistquaker.wordpress.com/2015/06/23/misunderstanding-forgiveness/.

63. Fox, *Journal*, 180.

64. *Sukla Yajur Veda* 36, in May, "06 hinduism+sky+bck," slide 132.

65. Ueshiba, *Art of Peace*, 121.

66. Laubach, *Letters*, 42–3.

67. Gautama Buddha, "The Metta Sutta, The Buddha's Teaching on Lovingkindness," https://shakyamuni.tripod.com/Sutras/metta_sutra.htm.

68. Betz Hall, *Forgiveness*, 1, 3–4, 18. Last ellipsis in original. Para. 4 ("Forgiveness means that I am no longer bound . . . ") is credited to Green and Grundy, *Matthew 18*, n.p.

69. Lamott, "Quote by Anne Lamott," https://www.goodreads.com/quotes/39817-not-forgiving-is-like-drinking-rat-poison-and-then-waiting. Cited to Lamott, *Traveling Mercies*, n.p.

70. Dalai Lama in Brach, "My Religion Is Kindness," https://www.psychologytoday.com/us/blog/finding-true-refuge/201506/my-religion-is-kindness, para. 1.

71. Eliot, "The responsibility of tolerance," https://libquotes.com/george-eliot/quote/lbg7ioe. Cited to Eliot, *The Mill on the Floss*, n.p.

72. Thurman, *Mysticism and the Experience of Love*, 20.

73. Raymond, *Rocking the Babies*, 133.

74. Penn, *Some Fruits of Solitude*, 154. Also available in Yearly Meeting of Quakers in Britain, *Quaker Faith and Practice*, entry 24.03. One might assume that Penn named Pennsylvania after himself, but in fact he chose "Sylvania," and it was King Charles II who insisted that "Penn" be included to honor Penn's father, Admiral William Penn.

75. Hạnh, *No Death No Fear*, 147.

76. Yungblut, *Hallowing One's Diminishments*, 5–6.

77. Romans 14:8. Adaptation by Shulamith Clearbridge from an amalgamation of versions, and changed into the first person singular.

78. Eckhart, *Meditations*, 199.

79. Yungblut, *Hallowing One's Diminishments*, 26.

80. Psalm 31:9–15. Combination of versions from NIV (available at https://www.biblegateway.com/passage/?search=Psalm+31%3A9–15&version=NIV) and Lamsa, *Holy Bible*, 601.

81. Ambler, *Living in Dark Times*, 25–26.

82. Rabbi Nachman of Bratslav, "Meditation for Rosh Hashona," in Stern, *Gates of Repentance*, 307. Online at https://archive.org/details/gatesofrepentanc0000unse.

83. Bahá'u'lláh, "Thy name is my healing, O my God . . . ," http://www.bahaiprayers.org/healing2.htm.

84. Omotoso, *Woman Next Door*, 118.

85. Spacey, "3 Origins," para 8. Spacey writes, "The 13th century Persian Sufi poet Suft Farid al-Din Attar of Nishapu recounted a fable of a king who asks a group of wise men for a ring that will make him happy when sad and sad when happy. The wise men debate amongst themselves and come up with the phrase 'this too shall pass.' This is the likely origin of the phrase."

86. "Multifaith Prayers," https://www.brighamandwomens.org/patients-and-families/spiritual-care/multifaith-prayers.

87. Weinstein, *The Better Man*, 203.

88. Psalm 147:3. Lamsa, *Holy Bible*, 658.

89. Vining, *Being Seventy*, 131–32. Also in Kenworthy, *Nine Contemporary Quaker Women*, 68.

90. Drayton, *On Living*, 29. In his book *Truth of the Heart*, Rex Ambler defines "Christ" as originally being a title given to Jesus of Nazareth, then it became a name both for the man Jesus and for the son of God who became human. Then Ambler says: "In Fox it nearly always carries this strong theological meaning: Christ is 'the word of God' or 'the light of God' by which God created the world and communicates with human beings, bringing them

to an awareness and experience of God. So in Fox, Christ can be said to be the source of creation itself and also the divine light in every human being." (Ambler, *Truth of the Heart*, 153)

91. Edelman, *Motherless Daughters*, 282–83.

92. Rilke, "#17," in *Sonnets to Orpheus*, n.p.

93. Stern, *Gates of Repentance*, 158.

94. Vining, *Being Seventy*, 168.

95. Clearbridge, *Plain Talk about Dying*, 2.

96. The Spiritual Life, "Native American Prayers and Blessings," https://slife.org/native-american-prayers/.

97. Burnell, in Yearly Meeting of Quakers in Britain, *Quaker Faith and Practice*, entry 21.66.

98. Vining, in Kenworthy, *Nine Contemporary Quaker Women*, 63.

99. "Maariv for Motza'ei Shabbat." Portions are from Psalm 29 (NLT), Psalm 30 (KJV), Isaiah 51:3 (KJV) and 57:19 (ASV), and many biblical references to God turning a curse into a blessing. Adapted by Clearbridge. This is from the opening prayer of the orthodox Jewish evening worship service at the conclusion of the Sabbath. Many Jewish prayers are amalgamations of psalms, verses, and ideas from the Old Testament of the Bible.

100. Edelman, *Motherless Daughters*, 13.

101. Vining, *World in Tune*, 97.

102. Braestrup, *Here If You Need Me*, 202.

103. Fox, *Journal*, 283–84.

104. ClevelandPeople.com, "Native American Indian Wisdom – Quotes and Proverbs," https://www.clevelandpeople.com/groups/amindian/amindian-quotes.htm.

105. Clearbridge, *Finding God*, 66.

106. Grou, *Hidden Life*, xiii, 135.

107. Loyson, "Family and Church," 113. Available online at: https://quoteinvestigator.com/2020/04/29/tree-shade/

108. Teresa of Avila, in Filz, "St. Teresa of Avila's Famous Poem," https://www.catholiccompany.com/magazine/nada-te-turbe-teresa-avila-poem-5760.

109. de Sales, in Women of Grace Staff, "We shall steer safely," https://www.womenofgrace.com/blog/79574.

110. *Sukla Yajur Veda* 16, in May, "06 hinduism+sky+bck," slide 131.

111. Clearbridge. Private conversation. 2004. Marjorie was a Quaker from Lake Forest Friends Meeting in Illinois.

112. Niebuhr, in Fred Shapiro, "You Can Quote Them," Yale Alumni Magazine, Jul/Aug 2010, https://yalealumnimagazine.com/articles/2926-you-can-quote-them. His 1937 version: "Father, give us courage to change what must be altered, serenity to accept what cannot be helped, and the insight to know the one from the other."

113. Niebuhr, "Reinhold Niebuhr quote," https://www.azquotes.com/quote/1446767.

114. Beck, *Expecting Adam*, 315–16.

115. Galilei, "2 November 1630," http://galileo.rice.edu/fam/letters/2nov1630.html. Quoted in Sobel, *Galileo's Daughter*, n.p.

116. Leslau, *African Proverbs*, 24.

117. Bialock, "Breathing Underwater" in Schulz, "Breathing Underwater," https://edgeofatlantic.com/2018/03/06/breathing-underwater-by-sr-carol-bieleck-rscj/.

118. Smith, *Meditation*, 150–51.

119. The Anglican Church in Aotearoa, *New Zealand Prayer Book*, 157. Also in Carpenter, "The Lake of Beauty," n.p. The New Zealand version and some online versions say: " . . . and Love himself . . . and catch his own likeness . . . " and in other versions it's written as "herself" and "her." I have changed it to "itself" and "its."

120. Clearbridge, unpublished journal, 2007.

121. Nayler, "What the Possession of the Living Faith is," in *Works of James Nayler*, 92. Online at http://www.qhpress.org/texts/nayler/possess.html.

122. Underhill, *Ways of the Spirit*, 71.

123. Ueshiba, *Art of Peace*, 96.

124. Rumi, in *Illuminated Prayer*, 64.

125. Stern, *Gates of Repentance*, 66. Slightly adapted and changed into the first person singular.

126. Rumi, in *Illuminated Prayer*, 98.

127. *Golden Girls*, "Guess Who's Coming to a Wedding?," September 21, 1985.

128. Whittier, "The Brewing of Soma," http://www.qhpress.org/quakerpages/qwhp/soma.htm. Written in 1872.

129. von Hügel, *Mystical Element*, 271. Online preview available at: https://www.forgottenbooks.com/en/books/TheMysticalElementofReligionasStudiedinSaintCatherineofGenoaandHerFriends_10057905.

130. Sutta 118, *Majjhima Nikaya*, §2, para. 4, Pali Tipitaka. Online at https://buddhamind.works/the-sutra-on-breathing/. Also available in Hạnh, *Awakening of the Heart*, n.p.

131. Penington, in Yearly Meeting of Quakers in Britain, *Quaker Faith and Practice*, entry 10.01.

132. Rohr, "The Art of Letting Go," adapted and transcribed at https://cac.org/daily-meditations/alternative-orthodoxy-week-2-summary-2016-02-20/.

133. Fell, "Letter to Col. William Osburne" (Letter 73), in Glines, *Undaunted Zeal*, 241.

134. de Mello, *Song of the Bird*, 163.

135. Tagore, *Gitanjali*, #XXXVI.

136. Kelly, *Testament of Devotion*, 45.

137. Penington, in Yearly Meeting of Quakers in Britain, *Quaker Faith and Practice*, entry 26.70.

138. Adapted from *Rig Veda* 2:28:1–9, in May, "06 hinduism+sky+bck," slide 123.

139. Woolman, *Journal and Major Essays*, 243.

140. These three queries come from Illinois Yearly Meeting, *Faith and Practice*, 36, 38.

141. Van de Weyer, *Celtic Praise*, 29.

142. van Balen Holt, *Dwelling Place Within*, 105.

143. Conger, *It's Probably Nothing*, xi–xii.

144. Tyson, in Yearly Meeting of Quakers in Britain, *Quaker Faith and Practice*, entry 10.18.

145. Kaufman, "Beneath the Purple Flowers," https://2008.dartmouth.org/s/1353/images/gid342/editor_documents/08_update_2_feb_09_comp.pdf?gid=342&pgid=61&sessionid=d325dffe-e852-4199-9aeb-cdc147fc1cc7&cc=1, para. 8.

146. Teresa of Avila, "No Wonder You Have So Few Friends!" https://www.adidaupclose.org/Crazy_Wisdom/teresa.html. Many versions of this story exist.

147. Nesbitt and Zimet, *A Tender Time*, 88–89.

148. Lord, "Prayer for Humility," https://www.ignatianspirituality.com/prayer-for-humility. Quoted in Harter, *Hearts on Fire*, n.p.

149. Mother Teresa in "Mother Teresa Says: 'We must not drift away from the humble . . . . ,'" https://wisebluesky.com/mother-teresa-says-we-must-not-drift-away-from-the-humble/. Also included in Mother Teresa, *Love: A Fruit Always in Season*, n.p..

150. Dickens, *David Copperfield*, 521.

151. Goudge, *Rosemary Tree*, 119.

152. The Holy Qur'an, "The Light," in Helminski, *Light of Dawn*, 24:36–8.

153. Confucius, *Analects*, 10. Book 1, passage 16.

154. Taylor, *Irish Country Village*, 353.

155. Beaver, "Quote by Jim Beaver," https://www.goodreads.com/quotes/9359243-no-one-is-completely-useless-you-can-always-serve-as. Cited to Beaver, *Life's That Way*, n.p.

156. Rumi, "Zero Circle," https://www.zharar.org/index.php?do=shorttexts&action=item&id=11026.

157. Woolman, *Journal and Major Essays*, 247.

158. Stern, *Gates of Repentance*, 3. Adapted. Quoted in Jill R. Hughes, "The Hand Before the Eye," *Foreword Reviews*, January / February 2000, https://www.forewordreviews.com/reviews/the-hand-before-the-eye/.

159. Tabor, *Four Doors*, 15.

160. Kabir, "XXXIV," in *One Hundred Poems*, 40.

161. Woolman, *Journal and Major Essays*, 247.

162. Mother Teresa, *No Greater Love*, 34.

163. Szekely, "God Speaks to Man," https://www.poetry-chaikhana.com/Poets/S/SzekelyEdmon/GodSpeakstoM/index.html. This poem is included in Szekely, *Essene Gospel of Peace*, n.p.

164. Living Hour, "Native American Prayers," https://livinghour.org/lords-prayer/native-american-prayers/.

165. Woolman, *Journal and Major Essays*, 88.

166. Illinois Yearly Meeting, *Faith and Practice*, 30, 36.

167. Chuang-tzu, in "A bit of philosophy," https://wileykit.wordpress.com/category/poetry, para. 3. This quote is included in Mitchell, *Enlightened Heart*, n.p.

168. Penington, "Some Questions and Answers," 344–345.

169. Lucas, "Sweet Hymns and Songs Will I Recite," https://hymnary.org/text/sweet_hymns_and_songs_will_i_recite. Originally written in 1914. Included in Stern, *Gates of Repentance*, 165, in the updated language used here.

170. Laubach, *Letters*, 47

171. Deuteronomy 6:5–9 (NKJV). Online at https://www.biblegateway.com/passage/?search=Deuteronomy+6%3A5-9&version=NKJV

172. Palmer, "Prayer for My Family," https://www.lords-prayer-words.com/prayers_before/family_prayer.html.

173. Tagore, *Gitanjali*, #LXIX.

174. Catherine of Siena, *Dialogue of Saint Catherine of Siena*, 27.

175. Uhlein, *Meditations with Hildegard of Bingen*, 92.

176. Adapted from multiple versions. Online versions omit various portions of this blessing. In an attempt to have most or all of it, I have included stanzas from Macleod, "Celtic Blessing of Deep Peace," https://hillsidesource.com/celtic-blessing-of-deep-peace and Macleod, "Deep Peace," https://www.godweb.org/prayerwave.htm, as well as Hennessy, "Deep Peace – An Ancient Celtic Blessing," https://insighttimer.com/DeeH/guided-meditations/deep-peace-an-ancient-celtic-blessing. The former two versions cite "The Dominion of Dreams Under a Dark Star," written by Macleod in 1895.

177. Ueshiba, *Art of Peace*, 181. "Vibrate" was translated as "echoes" but I think "vibrates" is a better choice for what Ueshiba means, based on what I have felt practicing aikido and in prayer.

178. Winterson, *Lighthousekeeping*, 196–97.

179. Mathias, "Holy Ground of Kalighat," https://anitamathias.com/2011/07/17/the-holy-ground-of-kalighat/. Quoted in Ford-Grabowsky, *Woman Prayers*, n.p.

180. Woolman, in New England Yearly Meeting, interim *Faith and Practice*, 144.

181. Derived from Yearly Meeting of Quakers in Britain, *Quaker Faith and Practice*, Advices and Queries #17.

182. Yearly Meeting of Quakers in Britain, *Quaker Faith and Practice*, Advices and Queries #17.

183. Yearly Meeting of Quakers in Britain, *Quaker Faith and Practice*, Advices and Queries #17.

184. Yearly Meeting of Quakers in Britain, *Quaker Faith and Practice*, Advices and Queries #26.

185. Illinois Yearly Meeting, *Faith and Practice*, 36.

186. The Holy Qur'an, "The House of Imran," in Helminski, *Light of Dawn*, 3:102–4

187. Clearbridge, "Evening Meditation," in *Finding God*, 65.

188. World Prayers, "*Oludumare*, oh Divine One!" https://www.world-prayers.org/archive/prayers/adorations/oludumare_oh_divine_one.html.

189. Gautama Buddha, in TransformationSeekersGuide.com, "Famous Quotes About Gratitude," https://www.practical-personal-development-advice.com/quotes-about-gratitude.html.

190. The Anglican Church in Aotearoa, "Night Prayer," in *New Zealand Prayer Book*, 183.

191. Prayer received through guidance, Clearbridge. Unpublished journal, 2007.

Bibliography

Adler, Herbert, ed. *Mahzor Avodat Ohel Moed—Avodat Yom haZikaron.* Translated by Arthur Davis. London: George Routledge; New York: H.D. Buegeleisen, 1907. https://opensiddur.org/?p=27332.

Adsit, Dennis. "The Real Lesson in the Taoist Farmer Story." New Ventures West. https://newventureswest.com/real-lesson-taoist-farmer-story/.

Ambler, Rex. *Living in Dark Times.* Pendle Hill Pamphlet 447. Wallingford, PA: Pendle Hill, 2017.

———. *Truth of the Heart.* 2nd ed. Philadelphia: QuakerBooks; London: Friends House, 2007.

The Anglican Church in Aotearoa, New Zealand and Polynesia. *A New Zealand Prayer Book / He Karakia Mihinare o Aotearoa.* Auckland: The Anglican Church in Aotearoa, New Zealand and Polynesia, 1988.

Bahauddin. *The Drowned Book: Ecstatic and Earthy Reflections of Bahauddin: the Father of Rumi.* Translated by Coleman Barks and John Moyne. New York: HarperCollins, 2004.

Bahá'u'lláh. "Thy name is my healing, O my God . . . ." Bahá'í Prayers. http://www.bahaiprayers.org/healing2.htm.

Beaver, Jim. "Quote by Jim Beaver." Goodreads. https://www.goodreads.com/quotes/9359243-no-one-is-completely-useless-you-can-always-serve-as.

Beck, Martha. *Expecting Adam.* New York: Times Books, 1999.

Betz Hall, Christine. *Forgiveness: Freed to Love.* Pendle Hill Pamphlet 480. Wallingford, PA: Pendle Hill, 2023.

Birkel, Michael. *The Messenger That Goes Before: Reading Margaret Fell for Spiritual Nurture.* Pendle Hill Pamphlet 398. Wallingford, PA: Pendle Hill, 2008.

"A bit of philosophy." Science, Creation and Imagination, October 31, 2012. https://wileykit.wordpress.com/category/poetry/.

Boyle, Gregory. *Tattoos on the Heart: The Power of Boundless Compassion.* New York: Free Press, 2010.

Brach, Tara. "My Religion Is Kindness." *Psychology Today,* June 17, 2015. https://www.psychologytoday.com/us/blog/finding-true-refuge/201506/my-religion-is-kindness.

Braestrup, Kate. *Here If You Need Me: A True Story*. New York: Back Bay Books, 2007.

Carpenter, Edward. "The Lake of Beauty." In *Towards Democracy*. Manchester: Labour, 1896.

Catherine of Siena. *The Dialogue of Saint Catherine of Siena*. Translated by Algar Thorold. London: Kegan Paul, Trench, Trubner, 1907.

Chouraqui, André. *Les Saumes: Louanges Traduction et commentaires d'André Chouraqui, Édition complète et définitive*. Paris: Éditions du Rocher, 1996.

Clearbridge, Barbara [Shulamith]. *Finding God: Prayers and Spiritual Practices from Many Traditions*. Port Townsend, WA: Peace Eagle, 1995.

Clearbridge, Shulamith. *Plain Talk about Dying: The Spiritual Effects of Taking My Father off Life Support*. Pendle Hill Pamphlet 479. Wallingford, PA: Pendle Hill, 2023.

ClevelandPeople.com. "Native American Indian Wisdom–Quotes and Proverbs." https://www.clevelandpeople.com/groups/amindian/amindian-quotes.htm.

Collins, Jon. "Voices: Henri Nouwen on Joy." *From Behind the Pulpit*, April 21, 2021. https://revcollins.com/2021/04/21/voices-henri-nouwen-on-joy/.

Confucius. *The Analects: Chinese-English Edition*. Translated by D.C. Lau. Taiwan: Linking Publishing, 2009.

Conger, Beach. *It's Probably Nothing: More Adventures of a Vermont Country Doctor*. White River Junction, VT: Chelsea Green, 2011.

de Mello, Anthony. *The Song of the Bird*. New York: Doubleday, 1982.

Dickens, Charles. *The Personal History of David Copperfield*. London: Bradbury & Evans, 1850. https://en.wikisource.org/wiki/Personal_History_of_David_Copperfield_(1850).

Drayton, Brian. *On Living With A Concern for Gospel Ministry*. Philadelphia: Quaker Press of Friends General Conference, 2006.

Eckhart, Meister. *Meditations with Meister Eckhart*. Translated and edited by Matthew Fox. Santa Fe, NM: Bear & Company, 1983.

Edelman, Hope. *Motherless Daughters: The Legacy of Loss*. Reading, MA: Addison-Wesley, 1994.

Elderton, Jono. "The Prayer of St. Richard of Chichester." Faith Hub. Great Life Publishing. https://faithhub.net/the-prayer-of-saint-richard/.

Eliot, George. "The responsibility of tolerance lies with those who have . . . " LibQuotes. https://libquotes.com/george-eliot/quote/lbg7ioe.

Filz, Gretchen. "Read St. Teresa of Avila's Famous Poem, in Her Own Handwriting." *Catholic Company*, October 14, 2025. https://www.catholiccompany.com/magazine/nada-te-turbe-teresa-avila-poem-5760.

Ford-Grabowsky, Mary, ed. *Woman Prayers: Prayers by Women Throughout History and Around the World*. San Francisco: HarperOne, 2003.

Foster, Richard J., and James Bryan Smith, eds. *Devotional Classics: Selected Readings for Individuals and Groups*. New York: Renovaré, 1993.

Fox, George. "Epistle 16." In "George Fox's Epistles." Richmond, IN: Quaker Bible Index, 2004. https://qbi.earlham.edu/gfe/e001–020.htm.

———. *The Journal of George Fox*. Edited by John L. Nickalls. Philadelphia: Philadelphia Yearly Meeting of the Religious Society of Friends, and QuakerBooks, 2005.

Galilei, Maria Celeste. "2 November 1630." Letters of Maria Celeste. The Galileo Project. https://galileo.library.rice.edu/fam/letters/2nov1630.html.

Gautama Buddha. "The Metta Sutta, The Buddha's Teaching on Lovingkindness." Buddhist Practice in Belgium. https://shakyamuni.tripod.com/Sutras/metta_sutra.htm.

Glines, Elsa F., ed. *Undaunted Zeal: The Letters of Margaret Fell*. Richmond, IN: Friends United, 2003.

Golden Girls. "Guess Who's Coming to a Wedding?" Season 1, Episode 2. Directed by Paul Bogart, written by Susan Harris. Aired September 21, 1985, on NBC.

Goudge, Elizabeth. *The Rosemary Tree*. London: Hodder & Stoughton, 1976.

Green, Connie, and Marty Grundy. *Matthew 18: Wisdom for Living in Community*. Pendle Hill Pamphlet 399. Wallingford, PA: Pendle Hill, 2008.

Grou, Jean Nicholas. *The Hidden Life of the Soul*. London: Rivingtons, 1870.

Hạnh, Thích Nhất. *Awakening of the Heart: Essential Buddhist Sutras and Commentaries*. Berkeley, CA: Parallax, 2012.

———. *No Death No Fear*. New York: Free Press, 2002.

Harjo, Joy. *Conflict Resolution for Holy Beings: Poems*. New York: Norton, 2015.

Harter, Michael, ed. *Hearts on Fire: Praying with Jesuits*. St. Louis, MO: Institute of Jesuit Sources, 1993.

Havel, Vaclav. "The Kind of Hope I Often Think About." In *Disturbing the Peace: A Conversation with Karel Hvizdala*. Translated and with an introduction by Paul Wilson. New York: Vintage Books, 1990, 181.

Heidish, Marcy. *A Woman Called Moses*. N.p.: Dolan and Associates, 2010.

Helminski, Camille Adams, translator. *The Light of Dawn: Daily Readings from the Holy Qur'an*. Boulder, CO: Shambhala, 2000.

Hennessy, Dee. "Deep Peace—An Ancient Celtic Blessing." InsightTimer. https://insighttimer.com/DeeH/guided-meditations/deep-peace-an-ancient-celtic-blessing.

Hughes, Jill R. "The Hand Before the Eye." *Foreword Reviews*, January / February 2000. https://www.forewordreviews.com/reviews/the-hand-before-the-eye/.

Illinois Yearly Meeting of the Religious Society of Friends. *Faith and Practice of the Illinois Yearly Meeting of the Religious Society of Friends*. McNabb, IL: Illinois Yearly Meeting of the Religious Society of Friends, 2020.

The Illuminated Prayer: The Five-Times Prayer of the Sufis as Revealed by Jellaludin Rumi and Bawa Muhaiyaddeen. Translations and commentary by Coleman Barks, illuminations by Michael Green. New York: Ballantine, 2000.

Jesuit Resource. "Native American Prayers." Xavier University Center for Mission and Identity. https://www.xavier.edu/jesuitresource/online-resources/prayer-index/native-american.

Kabir. *One Hundred Poems of Kabir*. Translated by Rabindranath Tagore and Evelyn Underhill. London: Macmillan, 1915.

Kaufman, Zak. "Beneath the Purple Flowers." *The '08 Update*. Dartmouth College, February 2009. https://2008.dartmouth.org/s/1353/images/gid342/editor_documents/08_update_2_feb_09_comp.pdf?gid=342&pgid=61&sessionid=d325dffe-e852-4199-9aeb-cdc147fc1cc7&cc=1.

Kelly, Thomas R. *A Testament of Devotion*. New York: Harper & Brothers, 1941.

Kenworthy, Leonard S., ed. *Nine Contemporary Quaker Women Speak: Margaret Bacon, Elise Boulding, Rachel DuBois, Elfrida Foulds, Helen Hole, Mary Hoxie Jones, Daisy Newman, Elizabeth (Gray) Vining, Elizabeth Watson*. Kennett Square, PA: Quaker Publications, 1989.

Lamott, Anne. *Traveling Mercies: Some Thoughts on Faith*. New York: Anchor, 2000.

———. "Quote by Anne Lamott." Goodreads. https://www.goodreads.com/quotes/39817-not-forgiving-is-like-drinking-rat-poison-and-then-waiting.

Lamsa, George M. *Holy Bible from Ancient Eastern Manuscripts*. Philadelphia, PA: A. J. Holman, 1957.

Laubach, Frank C. *Letters by a Modern Mystic: Excerpts from letters written at Dansalan, Lake Lanao, Philippine Islands to his father*. New York: Student Volunteer Movement, 1937.

Leslau, Charlotte. *African Proverbs*. Mount Vernon, NY: Peter Pauper, 1962.

Linn, Dennis, et al. *Sleeping With Bread: Holding What Gives You Life*. Mahwah: Paulist, 1995.

Living Hour. "Native American Prayers." https://livinghour.org/lords-prayer/native-american-prayers/.

Lord, Daniel A. "Prayer for Humility." Ignatian Spirituality. Loyola Press. https://www.ignatianspirituality.com/prayer-for-humility.

Loyson, Hyacinthe. "The Family and the Church: Advent Conferences of Notre-Dame, Paris, 1866–7." New York: G. P. Putnam & Son., 1870.

Lucas, Alice. "Sweet Hymns and Songs I Will Recite." Hymnary.org. https://hymnary.org/text/sweet_hymns_and_songs_will_i_recite.

Macleod, Fiona [William Sharp]. "Celtic Blessing of Deep Peace." Hillside Source. https://hillsidesource.com/celtic-blessing-of-deep-peace.

———. "Deep Peace." GodWeb. https://www.godweb.org/prayerwave.htm.

March, Michael K. "Quotations from St. Julian of Norwich." *Interrupting the Silence*, May 8, 2012. https://interruptingthesilence.com/2012/05/08/quotations-from-st-julian-of-norwich/.

Mathias, Anita. "The Holy Ground of Kalighat." *Anita Mathias's Blog on Faith and Art*, July 17, 2011. https://anitamathias.com/2011/07/17/the-holy-ground-of-kalighat/.

May, Dann. "06 hinduism+sky+bck." Slideshare, January 2010. https://www.slideshare.net/slideshow/06-hinduismskybck/44790442.

May, Gerald G. *The Awakened Heart: Opening Yourself to the Love You Need*. San Francisco: HarperOne, 1991.

McKelvey, Douglas Kaine. *Every Moment Holy: New Liturgies for Daily Life, Vol. 1*. Nashville, TN: Rabbit Room, 2019.

Mitchell, Stephen, ed. *The Enlightened Heart: An Anthology of Sacred Poetry.* New York: Harper Perennial, 1993.

Mother Teresa. *The Joy in Loving: A Guide to Daily Living.* Edited by Edward Le Joly and Jaya Chaliha. London: Penguin Books, 2000.

———. *Love: A Fruit Always in Season.* San Francisco: Ignatius, 1987.

———. "Mother Teresa Says: 'We must not drift away from the humble . . . '" Wise Blue Sky. https://wisebluesky.com/mother-teresa-says-we-must-not-drift-away-from-the-humble/.

———. *No Greater Love.* Edited by Becky Benenate and Joseph Durepos. Novato, CA: New World Library, 1997.

———. "Quote by Mother Teresa." Goodreads. https://www.goodreads.com/quotes/663294-god-doesn-t-ask-that-we-succeed-in-everything-but-that.

"Multifaith Prayers." Brigham and Women's Hospital. https://www.brighamandwomens.org/patients-and-families/spiritual-care/multifaith-prayers.

Nayler, James. *Works of James Nayler.* Vol. 4. Edited by Licia Kuenning. Farmington, ME: Quaker Heritage, 2009. http://www.qhpress.org/texts/nayler/index.html.

Nesbitt, Patricia M. and Kristin Camitta Zimet. *A Tender Time: Quaker Voices on the End of Life.* Sandy Spring, MD: Baltimore Yearly Meeting of the Religious Society of Friends, 2024.

New England Yearly Meeting of Friends. *Faith and Practice* (Interim). Worcester, MA: New England Yearly Meeting of Friends, 2015.

Newcomer, Carrie. *The Point of Arrival.* Bloomington, IN: Carrie Newcomer Music (BMI), BMG Chrysalis, 2019.

Niebuhr, Reinhold. "Reinhold Niebuhr Quote." AZ Quotes. https://www.azquotes.com/quote/1446767.

Nouwen, Henri. *Here and Now: Living in the Spirit.* New York: Crossroad, 1994.

Omotoso, Yewande. *The Woman Next Door.* New York: Picador, 2017.

Palmer, Julie. "Prayer for My Family." Lords-prayer-words.com. https://www.lords-prayer-words.com/prayers_before/family_prayer.html.

Penington, Isaac. "Some Questions and Answers, Shewing Man his Duty." *Works of the long-mournful and sorely-distressed Isaac Penington* [. . .], Vol 2. London: James Phillips, 1784. Richmond, IN: Earlham School of Religion Digital Quaker Collection, 2003. 321–63. https://esr.earlham.edu/.

———. "To Friends of both the Chalfonts." In *Works of Isaac Penington.* Vol 2. Glenside, PA: Quaker Heritage, 1994. 494–99. http://www.qhpress.org/texts/penington/letter25.html.

Penn, William. *Some Fruits of Solitude.* London: Headley, 1905.

Prejean, Helen. *Dead Man Walking.* New York: Vintage, 2011.

Raymond, Linda. *Rocking the Babies.* New York: Viking, 1994.

Rilke, Rainer Maria. *Sonnets to Orpheus*. Translated by David Young. Middletown CT: Wesleyan University, 1987.

Rohr, Richard. "The Art of Letting Go: Living the Wisdom of Saint Francis," disc 4. Sounds True: 2010.

Rubin, Theodore I. *Compassion and Self-Hate: An Alternative to Despair*. New York: Touchstone, 1975.

Rumi, Jalaluddin. "Zero Circle." Zharar, September 23, 2025. https://www.zharar.org/index.php?do=shorttexts&action=item&id=11026.

Schulz, Bill. "Breathing Underwater by Sr. Carol Bieleck, RSCJ." *Edge of Atlantic*, March 6, 2018. https://edgeofatlantic.com/2018/03/06/breathing-underwater-by-sr-carol-bieleck-rscj/.

Shange, Ntozake. *for colored girls who have considered suicide / when the rainbow is enuf*. London: Methuen Drama, 1992.

Shapiro, Fred. "You Can Quote Them." *Yale Alumni Magazine*, Jul/Aug 2010. https://yalealumnimagazine.com/articles/2926-you-can-quote-them.

Smiley, Jane. *Good Faith*. New York: Anchor Books, 2003.

Smith, Bradford. *Meditation: The Inward Art*. Philadelphia: J. B. Lippincott, 1963.

Sobel, Dava. *Galileo's Daughter: A Historical Memoir of Science, Faith and Love*. New York: Penguin Books, 2000.

Spacey, John. "3 Origins of This Too Shall Pass." *Simplicable*, August 27, 2023. https://simplicable.com/new/this-too-shall-pass.

Spickard Keeler, Janaki. "Misunderstanding Forgiveness." *The Quietist Quaker*, June 23, 2015. https://quietistquaker.wordpress.com/2015/06/23/misunderstanding-forgiveness/.

The Spiritual Life. "Native American Prayers and Blessings." https://slife.org/native-american-prayers/.

Sr. Dorsee. "The only way to pray is to pray . . . " *Witnesses to Hope*, June 14, 2011. https://witnessestohope.org/2011/06/14/the-only-way-to-pray-is-to-pray/.

Steere, Douglas V. *Traveling In*. Pendle Hill Pamphlet 324. Wallingford, PA: Pendle Hill, 1984.

Stern, Chaim, ed. *Gates of Repentance, The New Union Prayerbook for the Days of Awe*. New York: Central Conference of American Rabbis, 1978.

Stevenson, Robert Louis. "Like a clock during a thunderstorm." *Spiritual Quotes*, March 29, 2014. https://spiritual-quotes.org/enlightenment/like-clock-thunderstorm/.

Szekely, Edmond Bordeaux. *The Essene Gospel of Peace: Book two, Unknown books of the Essenes*. Cartago, Costa Rica: International Biogenic Society, 1981.

———. "God Speaks to Man." Poetry Chaikhana. https://www.poetry-chaikhana.com/Poets/S/SzekelyEdmon/GodSpeakstoM/index.html.

Tabor, William. *Four Doors to Meeting for Worship*. Pendle Hill Pamphlet 306. Wallingford, PA: Pendle Hill, 1992.

Tagore, Rabindranath. "The Child Angel." In *The Crescent Moon: Child-poems*. New York: Macmillan, 1914.

———. *Gitanjali (Song Offerings)*. New York: Macmillan, 1916.

Taylor, Patrick. *An Irish Country Village*. New York: Forge, 2022

Teresa of Avila. "No Wonder You Have So Few Friends!" *Adi Da and Adidam*. https://www.adidaupclose.org/Crazy_Wisdom/teresa.html.

Thurman, Howard. *Mysticism and the Experience of Love*. Pendle Hill Pamphlet 115. Wallingford, PA: Pendle Hill, 1979.

TransformationSeekersGuide.com. "Famous Quotes about Gratitude." https://www.practical-personal-development-advice.com/quotes-about-gratitude.html.

Tubman, Harriet. "Quote by Harriet Tubman." Goodreads. https://www.goodreads.com/quotes/22972-twant-me-twas-the-lord-i-always-told-him-i.

Twain, Mark. "Courage." TwainQuotes. http://www.twainquotes.com/Courage.html.

Ueshiba, Morihei. *The Art of Peace*. Translated and edited by John Stevens. Boulder, CO: Shambhala, 1992.

Uhlein, Gabriele, ed. *Meditations with Hildegard of Bingen*. Santa Fe, NM: Bear, 1982.

Underhill, Evelyn. *The Letters of Evelyn Underhill: Edited with an Introduction by Charles Williams*. Edited by Charles Williams. New York: Longmans, Green, 1944.

———. *The Ways of the Spirit*. New York: Crossroad, 1990.

van Balen Holt, Mary. *A Dwelling Place Within: Saint Francis of Assisi*. Ann Arbor, MI: Charis, 1999.

Van de Weyer, Robert. *Celtic Praise*. Nashville, TN: Abingdon, 1998.

Vining, Elizabeth Gray. *Being Seventy: the Measure of a Year*. New York: Viking, 1978.

———. *The World in Tune*. Wallingford, PA: Pendle Hill and Harper & Brothers, 1942.

von Hügel, Friedrich. *The Mystical Element of Religion as Studied in Saint Catherine of Genoa and Her Friends, Volume 1*. London: Forgotten Books, 1908.

Weinstein, Howard. *The Better Man*. New York: Pocket, 1994.

White, Lesli. "7 Daily Prayers For Women That Will Transform Your Prayer Life." Beliefnet (website). https://www.beliefnet.com/faiths/prayer/7-daily-prayers-women-transform-prayer-life.aspx.

Whittier, John Greenleaf. "The Brewing of Soma." Quaker Writings. http://www.qhpress.org/quakerpages/qwhp/soma.htm.

Winterson, Jeanette. *Lighthousekeeping*. London: Fourth Estate, 2004.

Women of Grace Staff. "We shall steer safely through every storm," Women of Grace, April 10, 2023. https://www.womenofgrace.com/blog/79574.

Woolman, John. *The Journal and Major Essays of John Woolman*. Edited by Phillips P. Moulton. Richmond, IN: Friends United, 1971.

World Prayers. "Oludumare, oh Divine One!" https://www.worldprayers.org/archive/prayers/adorations/oludumare_oh_divine_one.html.

The Yearly Meeting of the Religious Society of Friends (Quakers) in Britain. *Quaker Faith & Practice: the book of Christian discipline of the Yearly Meeting of the Religious Society of Friends (Quakers) in Britain*. 5th ed. London: The Yearly Meeting of the Religious Society of Friends (Quakers) in Britain, 2013.

Yungblut, John. *On Hallowing One's Diminishments*. Pendle Hill Pamphlet 292. Wallingford, PA: Pendle Hill, 1990.

First Line, Title, and Key Phrase Index

General Index

About the Author

Shulamith Clearbridge is a member of Swarthmore Friends Meeting in Pennsylvania, part of the Religious Society of Friends (Quakers). She is a writer, interfaith spiritual director, and workshop and retreat leader.

Her first book, published in 1995, was her MDiv thesis: *Finding God: Prayers & Spiritual Practices from Many Traditions*. Other books include *Recovery: Women's Words about Healing After Trauma* and the 2023 Pendle Hill Pamphlet *Plain Talk about Dying: The Spiritual Effects of Taking My Father Off Life Support*.

Shulamith has written numerous articles, both serious and humorous, for journals, newsletters, and newspapers. She has also written screenplays, short stories, poetry, and music. Shulamith has lived in the Philadelphia area since 2021, preceded by Vermont, New Zealand, the Olympic Peninsula, Canada, Seattle, and Chicago.

You can find Shulamith online at ClearBridgeToJoy.org.

PHOTO TAKEN AT PENDLE HILL, WALLINGFORD, PA

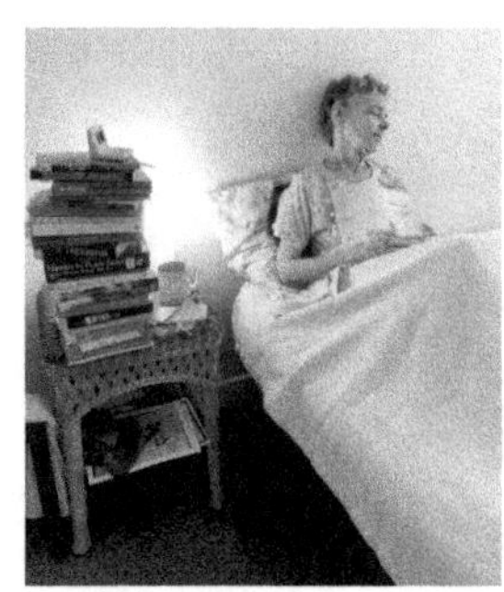

PHOTO BY SUE EDWARDS

www.ingramcontent.com/pod-product-compliance
Lightning Source LLC
LaVergne TN
LVHW050645100826
845148LV00011B/1996

* 9 7 9 8 3 8 5 2 6 9 3 2 7 *